ROUGH RIDER PRODUCTIONS
PRESENTS

STI...
Lets ...

G RATED

JOHN HELLMANN   BARNARD WHITE

And Rascal as "Rascal"

ALSO STARRING

QUINN WASHBURN
BILLY ROGER
DAPHNE DOODLE as "Little D"
KATIE I.
TEDDY T. GOOCH
ELAINE TRIGIANI as "Paradiddle"
And STEVE WILSON as "The President"

INTRODUCING ANTHONY R. BRILEY as "Nasty Sam"

Produced and Directed by GREY WHITTLE
Written by WILLARD KATZ and GEOFF RODGERS, based on a story by VIC TAIT
AND STEPHANIE SAMPSON AND STU CALEBESH & GREY WHITTLE

Music Adapted by Stuey Reed

Conducted by JEREOME NEWMAN
Animal training by STU'S FOUR-LEGGED HOLLYWOOD STARS
COLOR BY DELUXE

Novelization by JAMES TAYLOR JOHNSTON
Adapted from the screenplay by WILLARD KATZ and GEOFF RODGERS
Based on a story by VIC TAIT AND STEPHANIE SAMPSON
and STU CALEBESH & GREY WHITTLE
Character of Stinker created by BENJAMIN SILVER

INTRIGUE. SUSPENSE. ROMANCE.
TERROR. MYSTERY. MAGIC. CAR JUMPS.
EVEN SOME HUMOR!

Have you ever thought back on a movie—a specific scene or even the entire damn film—and wondered, *Did I dream that?*

This happens to me often. For years, I vaguely remembered watching a movie scene in which a young woman, wearing a black veil, strolls down a long line of soldiers and searches for just one volunteer.

No big deal. Won't just *one* soldier please volunteer? It'll be fun. You'll ride down an elongated slide with a giant razor in the middle, committing suicide.

I couldn't possibly have seen this, right? Well, yes. It turns out that I actually did see this. It was a scene from a 1964 movie, co-starring Sidney Poitier, about Moors and Vikings called *The Long Ships*, and I must have watched it on television in the mid-1970s and, not surprisingly, never forgotten it.

Watch it. The suicide scene—actually, more like a murder scene; the veiled woman *chooses* a soldier before he can officially *volunteer*—begins at the 1:14:30 mark. It's not as scary as I remember, although I still find it plenty disturbing. I'm still not 100% sure why the solider has to die.

Another movie I've often thought about over the years that I must have dreamt—I mean, *no way in hell could this possibly exist!*—is a film about a chimp in estrus and a dim-witted, cussing mountain boy who join forces with an out-of-shape Georgia road adventurer named Stinker so that they can "fun truck" their way up to Washington D.C.

Dear Lord! Could this possibly have existed?

Actually, yes. This film very much did exist. It was released in 1977 and played for a few weeks in theaters (mostly in the South) and in a few drive-ins (also mostly in the South).

The movie is called *Stinker Lets Loose!*

The movie is very bad. It will certainly never enter the lofty canon of the Criterion Collection, but I still remember it fondly. It was the first movie I ever saw in a theater—this would be in Virginia Beach—and I was five. Yes, *five*. I was with my parents, but still . . .

The movie would never—not for all the money in this ol' world—be made today. And yet I loved it then and I love it still. What can I say? I have a soft spot for movies that are very much "of their time," especially if that time took place in the 1970s. It's very hard to find a copy of this film beyond bootleg versions that were duped off VHS tapes that were recorded off cable (long after midnight) in the mid '80s to early '90s.

It's also surprisingly difficult to find *any* information on-line about this film. And perhaps that's for the best. To haul it all out into the direct sunlight, well, I don't know . . .

This book that you hold in your hands—this novelization to *Stinker Lets Loose!*—is the first in a series.

In the upcoming years, I will be re-publishing novelizations (or movie tie-ins) to forgotten films from the 1970s through the 2000s. Some of these will be about aliens. Some will be about virgins popping their "cherries" during spring break in that most exotic of party locales, Fort Lauderdale, Florida.

But a warning . . .

I'm publishing this book—as well as all the others— "as is."

That means that I haven't fixed so much as one word that was originally written by the authors that might possibly offend a reader on either moral or grammatical grounds.

James Taylor Johnston, the author of this novelization, died in 1987. Like the movie, it's difficult to glean any information about him or this book—although it wasn't for lack of trying.

The character of Stinker is described within these pages as "just the man this country needs in these difficult times." I tend to doubt that this was the case in 1977 and I most definitely doubt that this is the case now, and yet . . . there *is* something sort of refreshing about Stinker and his rag-tag group of "deep-fried Dixies."

And if you don't like Stinker or his story?

Well, what can I say? There are a lot of other great books out there, even a few great novelizations. Have you read the novelization to the 1979 comedy *The Fish That Saved Pittsburgh*?

It's terrific.

So, we'll talk soon. Until the next re-release, let me just say the following:

10-4, goody buddy! Keep the bugs off your glass and the trouble off your glass! Keep your lips a-smirkin' and the girls a-jerkin'! For sure, for sure! Catch you at the next Surf N Turf! . . .

MIKE SACKS

STINKER
Lets Loose!

Novelization by
JAMES TAYLOR JOHNSTON

Adapted from the screenplay by
WILLARD KATZ and GEOFF RODGERS

SUNSHINE BEAM PUBLISHING

NOTE: The characters and events in this
story are fictitious, but "The Scene" is not.

A SUNSHINE BEAM BOOK

Sunshine Beam Books are published by
Sunshine Beam Publishing, Inc, Hollywood, CA 90072

Design by Danielle Deschenes

First Printing, March 1977
Second printing, April 1977
Third and fourth printing, March 1978
Fifth printing, May 2017

PRINTED IN THE U.S.A.

Chapter 1

WAKEY, WAKEY!

Stinker opened his dazzling blue eyes, slowly and with great effort. He could barely see. Was it the middle of the night? No. It felt like daytime. Maybe late morning at the earliest. His eyes squinted from what little light invaded through the dirty, drawn shades.

A languid country song warbled from a radio-alarm clock. Not surprisingly, it was about Stinker:

> *That man, he like to ride,*
> *Ride, ride, ride . . . straight to his beer,*
> *That Stinker, he don't like to never, ever hide!*
> *This Stinker, he don't got at all nothin' to fear. . . .*

It wasn't a good song, nor did it make much sense, but until the day Stinker died—probably right here in his trailer, crushed under the weight of his vintage erotica collection—he'd be more than okay with it.

Stinker reached across his messy, stained, well-used mattress—over the box of wombat scat and around the jug of doe urine—for the radio's off button, hit it, and then accidentally knocked over an empty bottle of cinnamon whiskey. The sound of glass hitting and then

7

bouncing along the linoleum floor rang in his ears and made him wince. The label couldn't be seen, but it was the brand of cheap cooze-booze to be found at any illegal backwoods juke joint owned by a former career Navy cook named Gravy Boat.

'Twas the only style of booze Stinker ever drunk.

The great man now took stock of himself. He reached betwixt his thighs, making sure his ample package was still there.

There'd be a lot of upset ladies if it wasn't . . .

It was.

Good.

Rutting season would continue . . .

Stinker was "well-favored" by nature. The big trucker above had made sure of that!

Stinker giggled. The giggle was high-pitched, much like a jungle creature's. And extremely distinctive. Anyone who lived within the great state of Georgia knew this giggle, especially in the Southeastern part of Georgia, where Stinker resided and thrived.

"Moly holy! Where in the hell was I last night?" ejaculated Stinker, more to himself than to anyone else, as no one else was in the bedroom. "*Where now?*"

It started to slowly come back . . .

Ah, yes. With Lizzie . . . that spicy, slinky firecracker of an overnight waitress at Hank's Saloon . . .

That dirty little thang with the tight knockoff designer jeans. All moist around the edges . . . tea cup long since gone a'-cracked . . . slick in the sluice and dry in the goose . . .

And what did we do all night?

Got drunk and then . . . ahem.

That last part was best left to his own fading memory.

Where was Lizz now?

Not in this dump, that was for sure. She was a cat. Clean. Sleek. Stylish. Loved to lick. He was more like a dog. Smelly. Sometimes his penis was visible in public. Sometimes even his anus. He didn't care. Hairy.

Lizz's old man was a biker, which could spell danger: *Don't touch the snatch when daddy's got the patch* . . .

Not that Stinker was overly frightened. Cause Stinker had the *flesh*. Lived the *standard*.

The day was early yet but there was already a string of bubble gum lodged securely within Stinker's thick and lustrous 'stache. He'd have to attend to that later. Might even have to buy himself a monogrammed mustache wide-comb. Would go well with his monogrammed lice comb.

Stinker slowly made his way to a standing position. He was wearing nothing but his boxers festooned with the Confederate flag, and his authentic felt Stetson cowboy hat. *Always* with the cowboy hat . . .

"I'll be a dirty word!" he cried suddenly. "It's *you!*"

Sitting in a broken rocking chair, just next to the broken television, was Stinker's best friend and all-around loyal adventure comrade, Boner.

Unlike Stinker, Boner was clean-shaven and already duded up in his "Tuf-Nut Tux": crisp Levi jeans, mahogany red-supple genuine leather python cowboy boots with raised-topstitching, an antique pewter belt-buckle in the shape of an agave leaf, and a dark chocolate brown Biltmore Western cowboy hat raked handsomely to the side.

Southern exquisite. A denim dandy. A hoighty toighty honky-tonky cracker-backer slacker-wacker . . .

"Well, ain't you look like a hundred and ten bucks," Boner declared, smiling. It was an impish grin, one the ladies could never, *ever* resist. Even the guys had a difficult time ignoring it. Perhaps that had more to do with the discoloration of Boner's teeth and gums but Boner wasn't complain'.

"Smoke," declared Stinker, in a husky voice. "Need a smoke, pal."

Stinker tried to assume a frontiersman pose but nearly toppled over. He gave up and sat back down.

"Slow it down, jitterbug!" gibed Boner, laughing.

He tossed over a pack of fresh Salems. Stinker cooly caught the pack with one hand and then tapped out a "loose goose." He flipped it into his sensuous mouth. Boner blazed Stinker's cig and handed his best friend a pair of torn jeans and a denim shirt, the only style the great man wore. The shirt had a rhinestone peacock on the front giving the "middle finger." No one knew why.

Regardless, it was *glorious.*

"C'mon, friend," said Boner, pushing Stinker into the bathroom.

Boner had known this chaotic cracker for years and felt more than comfortable pushing Stinker into a trailer's tiny bathroom. "Your buddy is brewing up some strong joe, as well as a pipin' hot plate of hash."

He was talking about himself.

"Harumph," said Stinker, and then burped noisily.

Boner made a face. "You smell like the devil."

"The devil I know? Or the devil I don't?"

"Both," said Boner, even though he wasn't quite sure what Stinker meant.

He often didn't. But it didn't matter. They were best pals.

"Follow me, sir," said Boner, pretending he was a *maître d'* at a fancy, upscale French restaurant in the snootiest of academic northeast cities. He led Stinker out of the bathroom and over to the trailer's kitchenette area. "We saved your table, monsieur."

Stinker rolled his eyes. This was a game. Boner was forever playing the role of attendant, while Stinker was forever acting the role of rich, fancy gentleman. It was fun . . . but Stinker sometimes wished Boner could save it for another time. His entire body hurt!

Make no mistake, Stinker was in shape. But more like *beer shape*. He had some muscles but they were nothing to write home about.

Meanwhile, what exactly *did* Lizz and him get up to last night? Whatever it was, he was now paying the full price!

Stinker *hated* paying the full price.

Boner presented Stinker with a, steaming plate of delicious fried taters. He plunked down a huge cup of black coffee in a "SHIT KICKIN" mug, just the way Stinker *liked* it.

"Can't," said Stinker.

"Will," said Boner. "Don't let your alligator mouth overload your hummingbird ass."

Stinker took a deep gulp of the strong brew, and immediately began to feel better. "Where's Rascal?"

"Consumed by a croc?" asked Boner, handing Stinker a fake cloth napkin. "Ain't my chimp."

"That there's one animal who ain't gonna travel far," replied Stinker. "Not with that big, fat, lazy ass."

"She reached estrus last week," said Boner. "Going all types of crazy. Chimp lost her mind. Why *wouldn't* she run?"

Stinker retarted, "If she has run, I'm desiring she run off to find herself a male. And best of luck to 'im!"

Boner chuckled deeply and then sat down next to Stinker. All of a sudden, his expression showed one of deep concern. He remembered what he had to tell Stinker. And it wasn't good.

"Hey, buddy, I hate to be the barer of bad news and all . . ."

"Don't tell me," said Stinker.

Here it comes, thought Stinker. *A big roller-rink pickle.*

"I'm telling you," said Boner. "The Big Man wants to see you. Says it's of *mucho* importance. Has another job for you. Says it might be the most significant adventure of your already spectacular life."

"Of all days," said Stinker, anus puckering but not exposed. "Lord on a buttery shit biscuit, why today?"

Stinker's stomach grumbled and he floated out a lively one. A most dishonorable discharge. It smelled of government-issued hot dogs that had "turned" at a particularly depressing July 4th celebration.

"Helicopter is waiting," said Boner, holding his nose in a funny way and pointing outside to a large grassy area. "Been here for hours."

"Not going without Rascal," muttered Stinker. "No way, no how. That's a big *negatory!*"

"I wouldn't push buttons," said Boner. "Big Man sounded like he meant—"

There was a loud crash! Both Stinker and Boner jumped. Glass flew and the table was upended.

Before he knew it, Stinker was on the ground. Boner was still standing—*barely*.

"Speak of the devil I *know*," said Stinker, shaking his head. "There's my chimp now!"

Rascal the chimp roared with displeasure. Ever since she had reached sexual maturity the previous week, the great beast was capable of significant, ungodly violence. Grabbing the coffee pot, she hurled it against the refrigerator.

She bared her big, yellow fangs and then grabbed at her flap-jacked breasts and her freakishly inverted teats. She chewed at the air. She stomped and BM'ed on the cheap vinyl flooring.

The stinky soft-serve steamed profoundly *ferocious*.

"Madder than a tic in a tornado," exclaimed Boner. "Bitch chimp has two speeds: *violence* or *silence*."

Boner and Stinker threw back their heads and laughed uproariously. For Stinker, this was more fun than reciting dirty limericks while high on downers.

Yes, this chimp was off her rocker, there was no doubt about that! But there was also *something* about the old girl that was endearing. Maybe it was her loyalty. Or that she was always up for an adventure. Or good in a fight. Or free.

Stinker had stolen Rascal from an illegitimate traveling Injun circus in Alabama the previous month. And they were already fast friends.

Stinker wondered how this ol' chimp was going to do on a helicopter flight. She was scared to death of enclosed spaces. *Well, we'll soon find out,* he thought.

He closed his eyes and listened to the damage being wrought.

This should be fun.

Chapter 2

RECEIVIN' THE MARCHIN' ORDERS!

The Big Man stood before a seated Stinker. He didn't look happy. Which was nothing new.

"That's one hell of a monkey you got there, son," he said. "It really is *something*." The Big Man was seventy but looked no older than fifty.

Sixty at the tops.

Maybe mid-fifties if the lighting was good.

"Ain't a monkey," said Stinker.

He quickly added, "Sir."

Big Man couldn't tell if Stinker meant it or if he was just being country smart. Didn't matter either way.

"Either way, he creates havoc wherever he goes," said the Big Man.

Here we go again, thought Stinker, looking out the window, bored. This was a very powerful man who stood before Stinker. A powerful and dangerous man who had long ago become very rich by distributing convenience-store, barely-carbonated, corn-sweetened American-produced junk brew throughout the entire South. He had also somehow lost an arm. [See *Stinker Jumps the Grand Canyon with a Rented Jet Ski*, 1976]

So Big Man wasn't capable of adventures like he was back in his prime. But he was still exceedingly dangerous. And he hated animals. And the crippled.

And the Democrats.

Anything remotely vulnerable.

Life's a bitch, thought Stinker and snickered.

The Big Man pulled an expensive cigar out of an exotic cherry-wood cigar box with his good hand. "Care for one?"

"Why not?" asked Stinker. "Won't stunt my growth any."

Stinker gently took hold of the cigar and allowed Big Man to light him up. *Cuban,* Stinker thought. Stinker hated Communists, but oh boy, did he ever *love* that pinko backy . . .

"You're probably wondering why I called you here," said the Big Man.

"Had some curiosity," replied Stinker, tapping an ash out on his right leg, burning a hole right through the skin-tight, distressed denim.

He didn't care. *Plenty* of holes for everyone.

Stinker could see Rascal outside chasing the helicopter pilot 'round and 'round the chopper. *Don't get caught, Mr. Pilot. Don't you dare get caught!*

"I bet you're wondering, alright. You and I have been through a lot together, haven't we, Stink?"

I only allow my friends to call me Stink, Stinker thought.

And then aloud: "Sure."

"I ask and you do," said the Big Man. "I wanted a ton of beer delivered overnight to the Dallas Cowboys and you did that."

Yup, nodded Stinker.

"I need a hijacked shipment of fresh stool samples delivered to NASA, and you did that."

Stinker didn't remember this one.

"I wanted you to alleviate a sticky situation down at the new Disney complex and you did that."

"Still got the scars to prove it," said Stinker, smiling, pointing to his groin. "That's what I do, right? I'm a fixer. A deep-fried fixer who don't ask no questions."

"That's why you're the best," said the Big Man. "No one better. Here's the situation: I need you to personally deliver a six-pack of Schlitz to the President of the United States."

"The *President*?" asked Stinker, surprised.

"The one, the only," replied the Big Man.

"Why Schlitz and not Coors?" asked Stinker.

"You might not need to know that," said the Big Man.

"But how?" asked Stinker. "You know damn well that with my particular . . . past . . . I'm not exactly a *welcome* guest at the White House."

"That would be your problem," said the Big Man, now seated, genuine baby-elephant-leather boots up on his fancy chestnut-veneer work desk. "And that is why I'm paying you the big bucks."

He emphasized *big bucks* with his one good fore-finger.

"Speaking of which . . ." began Stinker.

"How's $10,000?" answered the Big Man.

"Might do," said Stinker. "Might not."

"Think it might," replied the Big Man, handing over a huge wad of cash. "Count it now. Go ahead. It's all there."

"I didn't say I'd do it," said Stinker.

"You didn't have to," said the Big Man. "I could read those big blue orbs of yours. All the evidence I need."

Outside, Stinker could see that Rascal had just ripped off the helicopter pilot's face and was now gorging on it as nourishment. *There goes my ride home*, thought Stinker and giggled.

"What's so funny, son?" asked the Big Man.

"Not much," Stinker replied, pointing out the window. "At least for *that* guy."

The Big Man didn't bother to look.

"So I suppose I could use the $10,000, yeah."

"I thought you would," replied the Big Man. "Still paying off that convertible Trans Am loan?"

Stinker stood. "By when?"

"Wednesday night. Or the deal is off."

"Wednesday!" screamed Stinker, who usually didn't scream. "That's impossible. Even for the Stinker!"

"Pluck me a sad song," declared the Big Man, mimicking the world's smallest banjo. "*Git*! And you owe me one helicopter pilot. See yourself home, please."

How in the hell did he know that his helicopter pilot was just eaten by a chimp without looking out the window?, thought Stinker.

Expensive video feed?

"And Stinker?" the Big Man continued.

"Yes?"

"God speed, son."

A scream could be heard from outside.

Stinker nodded.

"Impossible to find good help when you need it," mumbled the Big Man.

But he was only talking to himself. Stinker was already long past gone-gone.

Chapter 3

HITTIN' THE ROAD!

"He said *what*?" asked Boner, incredulous. "Impossible, chief! *Impossible*, I say, I say!"

"Ain't *nothin'* impossible," said Stinker. "Except for Buck speaking anything but a curse."

Stinker looked down at Buck, the wild-haired, whey-faced, small-eyed twelve-year-old he had illegally taken under his fry-battered wing the previous year whilst on a beer run in the mountains of Tennessee.

"Tit-*tays*," said Buck.

Stinker rolled his eyes. *Here we go.*

"Stanky starry hairy hole!"

"We don't use words like that," said Stinker, patiently. "It ain't *appropriate*, kid."

"Fuck," said Buck. "Fuck, shit, bitch, *cunt!*"

"Don't he say nothing but bad words?" asked Boner in genuine wonder. "Why he do that, son?"

"Been through it," said Stinker. "His first family was no good. Taught him everything that was bad. Our job is to teach him everything that's *good*. And I plan on it." He grabbed a beer from the fridge and tossed it to Buck.

"Consume it, kid. Will slow down those extra quick thoughts in that extra slow lil' mind."

The kid did as he was told. He adored Stinker.

"Getting back to the mission," said Boner. "Let's map out a plan here."

"Stinker don't map," declared Stinker. "The plan is simple: I jump into Miss Becky and get her all worked up. She scream with pleasure. She go *vroom-vroom*. You follow in that ol' stinking rig of yours. We reach the D of C in ten hours."

"Don't sound like a plan to me," said Boner.

"Cunt," said Buck, between sips. "Cunt, cock, piss, *shit!*"

"It's the only plan we got," said Stinker. "You got something better?"

"I'm afraid me thinks I doth not," said Boner, now acting all high-falutin', as if he were some sort of 19th century wench at a Renaissance Festival.

Stinker rolled his eyes but understood.

"I tell you what, ol' pal," said Stinker. "You go grab Jumbo. Tell him it's on. I and Buck will dig you by the Southside 95 ramp in T-minus sixty."

Stinker had *Go Fever* and it felt mighty good.

Grip it and rip it!

Holy hornies! This was *happening!*

"Time to go lookin' for trouble!" announced Stinker. "Cause we got ourselves engraved invitations!"

"Yeth, *thir*," said Boner. "Yeth, *thir*, commander!" He pretended to gayly salute like a homosexual soldier but instead stabbed himself in his right eye. It was funny and Stinker couldn't help but laugh.

"Pussy!" said Buck, taking a huge gulp of beer.

"C'mon, son," said Stinker slowly to the moronic mountain child. "Go get yourself dressed. Time for fun-truckin'."

Chapter 4

A RACK OF RIBBIN' WITH ALL THE SIDES!

One hour later, Stinker sat idling in his beloved Miss Becky, the convertible Trans he was still paying off in convenient monthly installments. Like the women he slept with, Miss Becky purred contentedly whenever Stinker stink-fingered her ignition.

Also, the car had a particular smell to her: *Cigarettes plus possibility plus hot cooter minus that "new factory smell."*

Sitting next to Stinker was the boy Buck, wearing a coonskin cap and old-fashioned motoring goggles. In the rear-view, Stinker noticed that Boner's truck was slowly approaching. He could just make out the "Big Mama"—Boner's 9-foot whip antenna—rapidly flapping in the wind.

After what seemed like eternity, Stinker could see the rest of the truck emerging from over the horizon.

In a short short, it arrived.

In the truck's passenger seat was none other than the fat man everyone called "Jumbo." He was large, had no job, and liked to go on exciting escapades. Truth be told, most of his brains was tightly packed into his jelly-stained Fruit of the Looms. He was sporting a stretched nylon nik-nik shirt with a beach sunset theme.

He smelled terribly of midnight masturbation.

He was a quivering heap of mother love, a simpering feeb. Stinker had known this fat slob ever since rescuing him from a dreary life cleaning the water flume at a South Carolina water park. Poor bastard was sleeping on a fetid cot 'neath Splish Splash Magic Velocity Mountain. He'd forever be in Stinker's debt.

"What's the news, Jumbo?" asked Stinker.

Jumbo laughed. He was forever laughing.

"See you haven't lost any weight," Stinker declared, popping a huge pink bubble.

Jumbo was not at all sensitive that he was a fatso. Or a glutton. Or a fool. He just wanted to have fun. *All* of the time. Jumbo would wink in an impish manner after telling a joke, as if to accentuate the mirth. He would laugh heartily whenever passing gas—which was often. Life was not a complicated spice ball of nuance for Jumbo. He provided comic relief, and Boner and Stinker found it all quite charming.

"I live to eat and I eat to live," responded Jumbo, in a jolly way. "Got any sweets?"

This was Jumbo's favorite line and he used it often.

"You know where you can find them sweets," replied Stinker. This was *his* favorite line. "Behind this big ol' mustache. Start diggin'!"

Jumbo burst out laughing. To Stinker, the laugh sounded just as loud and drunk as a donkey's.

You might be asking, *How did Stinker know what a loud and drunk donkey sounded like?*

As with everything, he just *knew*.

Also, he had recently forced at gunpoint a dwarf donkey named Gulliver to guzzle hard apple-cider at an unsanctioned New Orleans Halloween field party to the amusement of a large group of bikers and cancer-stricken children.

Gulliver died. As had most of the children. [See *Stinker and Gulliver Go A-Mardi-Gras'n*, 1974.]

"And we're off!" screamed Jumbo, raising an imaginary racing flag and waving it high and proud. He was like a killer clown, but without the makeup or wig. Or personality. He was balding and his left eye was sleepy-winky rheumy. He had dropsy and severe balance problems.

Boner popped the truck's clutch and the old heavy heap pushed slowly forward. He called his lovable rig the "Poon Goon," on account of the custom-built orgiastic sleeper cab with quadraphonic sound, orange rabbit-fur side-paneling, a small water bed that had long since run out of water, and a love mirror on the ceiling in the shape of a victory sign.

Women of a certain "type" found it "groovy."

Stinker and Buck, meanwhile, were already halfway down the road. Miss Becky was a mean, lean machine.

"Wait up, guys," screamed Jumbo from the truck, watching Miss Becky zoom off into the distance. He was pretending he was a giant newborn. "You just wait up! *Whaaaaaa!* I *waaaaant* my *Stiiiinker!*"

Next to Jumbo, Boner slapped in his favorite country 8-track, and the boot-scootin' swampy sounds blew forth nice and tangy.

This was Boner's theme:

Some people say that I'm just a deadbeat dad,
But the truth of the matter is,
I've only got the life they wish they always had . . .

Suddenly, and with no warning, a wild, high-pitched scream could be heard. And then another. The screams seemed to be coming from the truck's trailer where Rascal was tied down with circus chains. To Boner, these screams resembled screams of happiness. But you never knew. *You just never knew with that stolen bitch chimp in heat . . .*

Chapter 5

CALL IN THE TROOPS!

Somewhere between Georgia and Washington D.C., Clarence MacLeod sat alone on his leather throne, within his office, on the top floor of the tallest building South of the Mason Dixon. There was something off about Clarence. His momma used to call him "mean," but that was the least of it. His enemies liked to call him "evil," but even that didn't quite cut it. "Wicked" was the word Clarence preferred, and he supposed it was this word that was the most accurate.

"Rich" would be another word that could be used. The richest man in the entire South, if you must know. Except for the Big Man, who he hated.

"Stubborn" might be another description.

"Jealous," even another.

Maybe even "funny."

Perhaps "odd."

Clarence wouldn't argue with any of these descriptions. But he did hate the Big Man.

They had known each other for years and years. Grew up in the same small town of Greenwood, Mississippi, Clarence on one side of the great, raging river, the Big Man on the other. Despised each other *then*. Despised each other *now*.

Also, "tenacious."

Let 'em have their fancy words, he often thought. *Just let me at my money.*

Clarence pressed the large red button in the middle of his desk. A dial tone could be heard. And then a young woman picked up: "Yes?"

"Honey, it's Clarence. Get in here please."

"Yes, Mr. Clarence," said the youthful, sexy voice. "Right away, sir!"

Clarence leaned back in his leather chair and waited for the show to start. *Three, two, one . . .*

In walked Betty, strutting and sashaying like it was everybody's business.

Good Lord, Clarence thought. *Now that's one gorgeous piece of a—*

"Assignment?" asked Betty, taking a seat, cleavage confidently leading the way like two dowsing rods in search of the Lord's moisture. "New assignment?"

"Take this down," said Clarence, keeping his eyes on Betty's hefty honkers. "Stinker is out and about. He's on the loose and he needs to be stopped."

"Stinker?" asked Betty. She had once slept with Stinker. She smiled. Strong memories were now forming about Stinker's pungent womb-broom tickling her lady parts . . . that was *nice*. Smelled a bit like freshly mowed grass, with just a touch of unearthed manure.

Springtime.

"Come back, honey," said Clarence, annoyed. "Stinker has been hired to hand the President of the United States a six-pack of Schlitz. We can't let that happen. And do you know why?"

"Um, no," replied Betty. She had beautiful long hair and wasn't very intelligent, which wasn't a surprise. "I don't think so, no."

"Because we don't own Schlitz," said Clarence slowly. "We own Revive Beer."

"Revive, right," said Betty.

"And I hate Schlitz and I hate the Big Man. Starting to remember now?"

"Yes," said Betty, confused.

"Now what would happen to our sales if Stinker ever does happen to reach the President?"

"Down?" asked Betty, confused. "Go down?"

"That's right," answered Clarence, eyes still on Betty's generous ta-tas. The very last word on his mind now was "down," but he nodded regardless.

"Ah, okay," said Betty, pencil in her mouth, going in and out, in and out . . .

It was sexy.

Clarence thought for a minute. "Sweetheart, do you know what we have to do?"

It was more a proclamation than a question.

Betty again looked confused. It was a common look for her.

If her mind was as big as her assets, thought Clarence, *she'd take over the goddamn world . . .*

"Orville Max," continued Clarence, not waiting for the answer he knew would never arrive. "Orville Max *must stop* Stinker. Make it happen."

"Orville?" asked Betty. She had once slept with Orville Max. She smiled at the memory . . . tubs of melted margarine and homemade BBQ tongs.

Summer.

Clarence made a flick of his wrist to signify that the conversation was over. "Find Orville. Have him stop Stinker. Now get that pretty little behind in gear!"

Betty stood and Clarence waited for the second show to begin.

Here we go now, thought Clarence. *Three, two, one . . .*

Betty sashayed back through the office's door.

She didn't disappoint.

She never did.

Chapter 6

A BUZZ OF THE FUZZ!

"10-4, good buddy," Stinker barked into his custom gold-plated CB handset. In fancy cursive across the side, it read "Le Stinker."

"This here be the Stinker! Your number one Beaver Cleaver. Come back?"

Stinker fiddled with the channels and waited for a response. His channel was 69 and every gear jammer worth his salt lick knew it.

"Breaker for the Stinker," said a voice. "This here be the Plastic Duck."

"Go ahead, Plastic Ducky," said Stinker, smiling.

This should be good.

"We got a smokey on the move with the hammer down and the candles lit."

Stinker stopped smiling. The last thing he needed now was to be slowed down on his mission to deliver Schlitz to the President of the United States by a Johnny Law with a junk-buzzard mentality.

"Read that," replied Stinker. "Loud and clear."

"Hold onto your mudflaps, I ain't done," said Plastic Ducky, with laughter in his voice. "You have a sweet-looking beaver just about to pass. She got a short skirt and tasty seat covers. Driving a solid black Nipper Ripper. Ten bye-bye."

"10-4, Duck. Keep the bugs off your glass and the trouble off your glass," spurted Stinker.

"Keep your lips a-smirkin' and the girls a-jerkin'," responded the Plastic Duck.

"We be toppin' the hills and poppin' the pills! *Skin* it back and *squeeze* it down!" replied Stinker, but the Duck was already long past bye-bye.

Oh well.

Stinker placed the gold-plated handset back into the cradle of the Courier Conqueror 40D, the newest and most complicated of all CB transmitters. It had a digital alarm clock and an AM/SSB Transreceiver. It's slogan was "Tomorrow's CB Today."

Stinker couldn't imagine communicatin' ever getting better than this . . .

"Bitch," said Buck, in the bucket seat next to Stinker. "Bitch, bitch, bitch, *bitch*!"

"Let's just see about that," answered Stinker, looking in his side rear-view. "Patience, son. Here she comes now. Blowin' past like a 10-11 in the wind. I got me some beaver fever and a hot crotch with very little conscience! It's time to go spelunkin' for paddy pelt!"

Stinker and Buck watched the Jap-produced Toyota Celica speed past.

Stinker was surprised the car wasn't yellow.

Stinker estimated that the Nipper Clipper had to be zooming into the low 100s.

Easily.

"Lord now!" said Stinker. "Just sawn her! What a bra buster!"

Stinker picked up the custom gold CB handset again. "Breaker, breaker. C'mon in, Boner! Got us a real—"

But before he could finish his transmit to Boner, the sound of a police siren could be heard.

"Flies on a rib-eye!" screamed Stinker, who didn't often scream.

He pulled Miss Becky over to the side of the road, handling her better than any other man alive.

He kept the engine on. *You never knew.*

"Don't say nothin'," said Stinker, looking over to Buck. "I still don't got the proper papers for you. That's all I damn god need."

"Screw," said Buck.

"Screw is right," said Stinker. "Donut patrol always repossessin' my dreams!"

He waited for the inevitable window knock. Within seconds, it came.

"Anyone home?" asked the smokey, finger tapping on Stinker's window with its huge brass ring.

Stinker rolled the window down . . . *real* slow like.

"Stinker's home," replied Stinker. "And who may I ask is calling on this gorgeous, sunny day?" He was furiously chewing bubble gum. The cheap pink variety. The only kind worth blowin'.

The sheriff blushed a deep red. Packed in his lower lip was a plug of chaw. He was a large man, as wide as he was tall. He was Grade A by the books with a military bearing that screamed Hanoi. Stinker guessed the man had seen bookoo action. But nothing like the action Stinker had seen stateside.

"Well, that would be me! *I'm* the one calling!" said the smokey. "My name is John R. Sledge. That is . . . *Sheriff* John R. Sledge."

"And his partner, Pip!" announced a tiny voice.

Stinker looked puzzled. He scrunched his brow. Now where was *that* coming from?

"From down here," answered the voice, almost as if it could read Stinker's mind, which was impossible. *No one* could read Stinker's mind. Even Stinker.

Stinker stuck his prominent head out Miss Becky's window and looked down. He might as well have been gazing at a worthless insect. "Why, ain't you the cutest!" he chortled. "You ain't nothin' more than an itty bitty banty rooster!"

"I'm a man and I wish to be treated like one," squeaked the little man, adjusting his child-size sheriff's hat.

"Sure you do," giggled Stinker. "You're what my Mema would have called a knee-high shit-kicker with a regular-sized attitude!"

"Shit kicker," repeated Buck, laughing. "Shit kicker! Shit kicker! *Shit kicker!*"

"Now hold on just a minute, boy," said the sheriff to Stinker. He spit out a thin stream of dip that splash-splashed betwixt his expensive leather boots (bald eagle, endangered).

"That's my son you're talkin' 'bout here. He ain't tall but he sure can handle himself with a weapon. Ain't that right, boy?"

"You got that right, daddy," said the tiny man, puffing out his miniature chest. Stinker guessed he was no older than twenty-one or twenty-two. Stinker was wonderful with ages, most typically of the young, female variety. But this one . . . this one was like nothing he'd ever witnessed. A man child. A freak baby. A real ankle biter, by the looks of it.

"I ain't got time to chat," said Stinker, glancing at the digital clock on his CB transmitter. "Got a delivery to make. With the President of the United States!"

Stinker pointed to the back, at the emptied cardboard diaper box that held the specially gift-wrapped six-pack of Schlitz.

"That so?" asked the sheriff, not impressed. "Well, before you head on up to Watergate City, I'm afraid I gotta hand over a tick-tick for speeding."

"A bear bite," muttered Stinker.

"Whatever you want to call it, boy. You well over a century."

"*Over one hundred?*" asked Stinker, who was usually bear proof. "You confusing me with that tasty little Betty who breezed past just ahead. Jap jeep. Bazunkas out to *here*." Stinker spread his arms out wide, and then kept spreading them for comic effect.

"Jap, Jap, *Jap!*" screamed Buck.

"You calling me a liar, son?" asked the sheriff. He appeared none too pleased, even though he was suitably impressed with the size of this Betty's bazunkas.

"Hang on a split-second there, Johnny Law," said Stinker, picking up the CB mic. "Boner? Boner, c'mon in now!"

There was a squawk from the CB radio. "This here be the Boner," announced Boner, eventually. "Comin' up your stern side real soon. Meet ya at the next Surf N Turf!"

"Sounds good, ol' boy," said Stinker. "But I could use me some help first. You ready for a love tap? Got a care bear telling me things I ain't appreciatin'."

"A love tap!" yelled Boner. "Now you know I'm *always* in the mood for a love tap!"

Stinker thought: *Low pay. No job security. Danger at every turn. Trailer-truckin' was a disease. But it was also the cure. Was there any job on this here earth better than making a living on the road? Don't have to wait for no whistle to blow. The modern-day cowboy. Like a rabid dog who don't need no food or water. Just chasing that beautiful dream down America's red, white and blue highway and never stoppin', except for that inevitable road tang . . . and lizard lot gonorrhea . . . fer sure, fer sure . . .*

"Righto," said Stinker, all smooth. "We got the hammer down and we're motorin'!" He placed the CB mic back into its special cradle. Smiling wide, his mustache glistening with morning dew and perhaps a devil's dab of leftover "woman dew" from the previous night, he proclaimed, "Now what were you saying . . . sir?"

Oh, this'll be good, thought Stinker. *How I missed this.*

"What I was saying was that if I ever again catch you speeding, your ass will be grass."

The sheriff paused for effect and then continued: "And I'm the *lawnmower*—"

Just then a tremendous horn blasted from a big rig diesel. A K-Whopper by the sounds of it. Stinker knew who was responsible.

Who else? Boner!

The sheriff and the little man tried to jump out of the way. But it was far too late. The bundled-out freight-shaker and slicked-up moonraker was barreling down *way* too close, within just inches of Miss Becky.

Boner sure can ride, Stinker thought. *A true Honky Hercules! A goddamn tricky truckologist!*

The sheriff and his son threw themselves over to the side of the road and landed in a huge puddle of mud. Or was it manure? It was funny because both the sheriff and the tiny freak had been wearing all white. Now they were covered from head to toe in brown!

"Shit is the *perfect* color for you two!" screamed Stinker, gently popping Miss Becky's throttle into DRIVE and peeling away, sending up a rooster tail of gravel. Just the way she *liked* it. "Bye bye, boys!"

"You ain't experienced the last of us two!" screamed the tiny man, up to his knees in the nasty sick. He tried to wipe the ungodly vile from his eyes but couldn't, which made it all the more hilarious.

"We'll see about that!" cackled Stinker. His voice echoed as the Trans *vroomed* down the road. He knew damn well that he had just experienced the last of these two losers.

Didn't have to worry about them no more.

No way. No how.

The tiny man began to cry. His father, the sheriff, also began to cry. Two tough *smokey jokeys* crying their dirty eyes out.

The irony was yummy.

"Yahooo!" screamed Stinker.

"Fuck!" screamed Buck.

Steak and lobster awaited them all at the next truck-'em-up. The choke and puke was about 20 miles down the road.

Miss Becky knew the way.

Chapter 7

ORDERING OFF MENU!

Jumbo was holding court at Ma's Dixie Easy Travelin' Plaza, much like a jester would in France one thousand years ago.

Shirtless, with fat dribbling over his cut-off jean shorts, wearing a red-white-and-blue headband, Jumbo danced and sashayed and can-canned atop the Formica diner counter to the delight of the horde of truckers and other assorted grizzly sizzlies there to eat steak and lobster and Ma's world-famous apple pie, each slice topped with a perfectly scooped mound of American-produced vanilla ice cream. Stinker would have slept with Ma but she was old and, quite frankly, hideous. Ma reminded Stinker of something you might see on a bed of ice in Chinatown.

The diner was packed.

One trucker wore a T-shirt with a press-on decal of the Liberty Bell riding a dune buggy. Another wore a T-shirt with an image of a smiling Mexican with a gold tooth and a sombrero that read: *Acapulco Gold!*

In each hand—in each sweaty, *swollen* hand—Jumbo clutched a small American flag. Jumbo was huge and gross but you could never say that he didn't love America.

This bloated freak was definitely in his element.

"Land of the free, home of the brave," Jumbo sang to the tune of "America, the Beautiful." "I may be fat but I ain't a *slave!*"

The truckers roared their approval. Boner and Stinker smiled. You could take this load of lard anywhere and he'd *always* make friends. Even Buck was clapping his hands perfectly in time to the song, which was highly impressive, considering he was most likely brain damaged.

The kid was dragging on a Pall Mall, all cool like.

This twelve-year-old sure could smoke . . .

"Land of the free, home of the *bra!*" Jumbo sang.

The crowd—*Jumbo's* crowd—roared their approval. One gave a thumb's up. Another the victory sign. It was difficult not to feel patriotic with the bicentennial just having come and gone. If you didn't, there was something mentally wrong with your brain.

Jumbo was kicking his legs like a New York City Rockette during the Christian holiday season. "Just check out these gams!" he screamed, pointing to his pasty white legs.

And then, even louder, in a husky voice, Jumbo sang: "For the dear ol' flag. O, it brings me such peace and joy! Because this dear old flag—"

"Don't you mean *fag*," came a voice from the back of the diner. It wasn't even a question.

A trucker with long, greasy hair—and wearing a Civil War Confederate hat—leaned against the jukebox. He seemed to be the only one who wasn't having much fun.

There's always one, thought Stinker. *Always one . . .*

"Well, that's just about the most faggoty thing I ever did see," continued the man. "And I've seen a lot of faggoty things! So *many* faggoty things! Too many faggoty things to *count*! *Millions* of faggoty things!"

The man smiled, and yet it was obvious he regretted saying that last part aloud. Perhaps he could have phrased the entire statement a little better?

But it was too late now.

"Yeah, that sure was a real *treat*," he continued, a little softer.

When he emphasized *treat*, spittle flew from his mouth.

The noise level of the crowd abruptly fell to a hush-like whisper.

"You got a problem with my good friend?" asked Stinker, silver monogrammed toothpick bopping up and down in his enormous, sensuous mouth. "Cause I don't take too kindly to people who ain't too friendly to my friends."

"Maintain," muttered Boner, who was standing next to Stinker. "Not worth the goshdarn trouble it's written on. Likely swooping off barley wine. You got a President to meet, son. A dang ol' *President*!"

"I asked if you had a problem with my good friend," said Stinker, not letting it drop.

No one talked to his friends like that, even if they *were* kind of faggoty.

"Didn't know tough guys were friends with *faggots*," hissed the man in the Confederate hat. This was getting strange. There was trouble in the air. Jumbo could smell it, just beneath the smell of Ma's famous cheap chucks sizzling on the grill, all hot and blackened. People called them "Up Chucks." They did smell awful good, though.

The lobsters in the tank, on the other hand, smelled

very bad. Boner wondered if perhaps the tanks should contain water and not just street gravel.

Jumbo did a spastic little dance to show that his arms were thick and chunky. Some in the diner laughed. Most didn't. The mood had already been killed. Which was a shame. Jumbo carefully climbed down from the diner counter and stood off to the side. He wasn't a fighter. The show was over and he was famished.

Time for a self-applied chocolate enema.

"Need I repeat myself?" asked the man in the Confederate hat. "Or are y'all too pansy to answer?"

"Oh, I think I already gave my answer," replied Stinker, walking without hurry toward the man.

"I didn't hear it," said the man, not moving.

"How about now?" asked Stinker, raising up a pool cue, which was strange. The diner had no pool table.

Stinker swung the cue straight down onto the man's Confederate hat. There was a dull *thud*—to Boner it sounded almost as if a watermelon had just been dropped off a tall building by a trucker attempting to impress a Memphis whore—and within no time, the man in the Confederate hat had crumpled to the diner's floor, bleeding profusely and seemingly expired.

"Now, now," said another large man, placing his cheeseburger on a plate and standing up from the counter. The ashy dingleberry was wearing a Caterpillar trucker's cap. He wiped his chin with a cloth napkin that Ma was world-famous for—they were the *softest*.

"That wasn't a smart thing to do. Because that was *my* good friend," the man in the hat continued.

Turkey, thought Stinker. *World's biggest stuffed turkey!*

The large man had many tattoos. 'Twas tattooed from arsehole to breakfast time. From nose to hose. Most of his tattoos were swastikas, which usually signified danger. And racism.

Stinker hated a lot of things in this big ol' world.

But what he hated most of all was . . . *hatred*.

Just despised anyone who didn't love and respect anyone else who might look and act the tiniest bit different.

Stinker hated that more than *anything*.

Except blacks.

"Looks like we're about to play ball," said Boner to Stinker, who shrugged.

"Just another day at the office," said Stinker, his body coiling like a king cobra with a beer belly. "Ass, grass or *cash*. Nobody rides for free."

The first punch was delivered straight down the middle. The fight was on.

Chapter 8

A FRIENDLY STOP!

The fight was over.

The gang was back on the road, tooling down the four-lane stretch of asphalt toward a future only they could envision.

Stinker's mind wandered back to what had just happened. The fight hadn't started off well. The man with the swastika tattoos had been a solid puncher—this definitely was *not* his first diner fight—and he had gotten in plenty of robust licks that Stinker, Boner and the rest of the crew were still feeling.

Stinker had fought back valiantly, as had Boner. In the corner, Jumbo was asleep atop the *#1 American Champion Evel Knievel!* pinball machine. A small dollop of whipped cream covered his left eye. Dreaming about marshmallow clouds and vanilla rainbows, no doubt. Riding strawberry unicorns through fields of hazelnut candy corns. Stinker tried to think of more edible and food-based fantasy-land scenarios. He could only envision Jumbo petting a chocolate-mint squirrel with two misshapen peanut M&Ms for testicles, but that image wasn't exactly jibing.

Buck, using his arms as batons, had conducted the fight as one would an orchestra. A little more kicking *over here*. And a little more punching *over here*. It was funny and if Stinker hadn't been trying his best not to die, he would have laughed. Maybe he had. He couldn't remember.

Then the fight had taken a turn for the *strange*.

Rascal the chimp had unexpectedly appeared through the diner's front glass doors—literally *through* them—and had wasted little time in creating great destruction, ripping apart faces and arms and legs and, in one case, a giant toe belonging to a traveling belt-buckle salesman.

Rascal's strength was enormous. Estrus would do that to any chimp. And Stinker was happy for it. And responsible. He had let the ol' girl out of her circus chains. So maybe Rascal's appearance hadn't been so unexpected after all.

Even lady monkeys ain't easy when it's "that time," Stinker had thought as he watched in wondrous fascination.

Females are one hell of a complicated species!

But then, within moments, things had turned . . . even *stranger*.

Had there really been a food fight? thought Stinker. *Pies and cakes and even custard?* Or had Stinker imagined *that*? No, he had *not* imagined that. Or maybe he had. It was difficult to tell sometimes, this blurring of life and dream. Too many beers could do that to any man. And Stinker was up to his sixth in just the past few minutes. He was forever thirsty.

Stinker turned to Buck who was sleeping in the passenger seat, legs twitching. Kid was no doubt dreaming about visions only a subnormal twelve-year-old holler hillbilly would ever dream about: most likely teasin' creek turtles and setting fire to tipplehouses.

I'm lucky, thought Stinker. *This is the good life.*

And it was. True, Stinker knew a lot more people with a lot more money. With bigger trailers that had working toilets. With vasectomy scars created by licensed physicians. With cars that weren't nicknamed after deceased Memphis whores.

But Stinker had his goddamn freedom.

And wasn't that worth a lot more than *any* amount of money? Even the $18,000 he would have been earning each and every year by illegally hauling "gently used" dental supplies state to state?

Yeah, this was the good life, alright. The only thing Stinker now needed was a beautiful woman, and where on Lorne Greene's Earth could he ever possibly hope to find—

"Well, lo and behold!" screamed Stinker. He usually didn't scream. Or use the word "lo."

Buck awoke with a start.

"Fuck?" the boy muttered groggily. "Piss, fuck, *pussy*?"

"Go back to sleep, kid," said Stinker. "This is a *grown* man's business."

Miss Becky swerved over to the side of the two-lane highway just behind the stalled Toyota Celica with its hood up. Stinker recognized the car. It belonged to that gorgeous Betty from earlier, whizzing along, without a care in her cottony, pink-encrusted world.

Typical woman, thought Stinker. *Don't know a slipper piston from a tire thumper . . .*

And yet Stinker remembered catching just that fleeting glance when she had passed him doing at least 100. Those breasts! And that hair! Holy god on a barbecued bun! Stinker hadn't seen a female specimen this fine since . . . well, a few nights ago. But like any male lioness prowling the African sarangetti for sex, Stinker was *always* hungry.

"You called A.A.?" proclaimed Stinker, as he exited Miss Becky and made his way over to the Toyota. "Oooh-weee! I meant A.A.A.! *Watchout now!* I think I might just be the man to help!"

"I do need help, *thank you,*" said the voice still hidden behind the hood, absentmindedly.

This gal—she was *used* to getting her way!

"Well, let's see what we can do here, little lady," declared Stinker, adjusting his mustache, which sometimes pointed in all directions but the correct one. Stinker preferred it combed down.

He was no satin disco star.

Stinker still had a long strand of pink bubble gum lodged in his "molestache's" dense fur, and perhaps even a Cheerio back from snack time. And for some reason a match head. But it was too late to do anything about that now. He'd worry about all this at the next rest stop when he'd pay a Spanish to clean it for him.

Stinker quickened his pigeon-toed booted step and walked around the woman's stalled car . . .

BAM!!!!

And there she was. Before his very eyes.

He now saw, for the very first time in his life, what beauty—*real* beauty and not *dolled-up* beauty —looked like close-at-hand. He sized her up as if she was a pedigreed colt at a minimum-bid auction.

The lustrous devil hair on his knuckles began to quiver.

Sweetest piece of flesh he'd ever seen.

This was no Jezebel whore, a cherry without the stem.

No, this was a *lady*. As refined as they came. She was a slender filly! Solid teeth. Strong legs. Ropy, sturdy arms. A nice healthy color to her cheeks. Thoroughbred from top to bottom—*especially* the bottom. A clean, rural smell, like the goat-feed dispenser at Mema's farm. If Stinker ever decided to procreate, this champion mare would produce a most dynamite pinto.

And that meant the world. Not just to Stinker. But to the world.

Turning his attention to the engine, and trying his very best to act professional, Stinker declared, "She's surely busted. Sorry. You'll have to join us in our vehicle, ma'am."

"Your vehicle?" the woman asked, perplexed. "But didn't you say you were from A.A.A.? You're not here to help?"

"Ma'am, I just lied," said Stinker, taking off his cowboy hat and placing it over his heart. "But it's been a mighty long while since I've seen anyone so gosh-darned beautiful, and I do reckon that it would be best for all of us if you joined my boy and I on our adventure."

"And what adventure might that be?" asked the woman, adjusting her hot-pink jumpsuit, purchased at Fredericks of Hollywood—and not on credit.

"Ever wanted to meet the President of the United States?" replied Stinker, already knowing the answer.

"Thought about it," said the woman.

"Then come with me," said Stinker, "and so you shall." He extended his hand, much like a rich count would in 14th century Australia.

"Well . . ." began the woman.

Stinker got serious. "In life, you're either running *away* from something or *to* something. Which one for you?"

The woman looked into the face of this gorgeous man with the mustache as thick as a mound of hay at a chili fest. She saw sadness. And goodness. And a street wiseness she never in a million years could have learned at any liberal northeast fancy college.

Also, that one match head.

"*Away*," she finally replied. "My parents wanted me to marry the wrong man for all the wrong reasons. He's weak. But rich. And I like strong. And poor. Or lower-middle-class, anyway."

"I know," said Stinker, grinning. "I knew that from the start."

"And so I bought this car but . . ." she paused. "I don't know all too much about cars."

"Didn't think you would, honey," said Stinker. "Women drive cars like men change diapers. Messy and with god's guacamole a-flyin' a-hither and a-thither!"

"Besides," he continued, not receiving the response he was looking for. "This car ain't nothing but a heap of Jap crap. Oriental cheese. Won Ton phooey. Chink chintz. Stick to *American* made next time. And you can never go wrong."

Stinker pronounced the word *Amer . . . I . . . Can.*

It was impressive.

Stinker extended his left hand. Now he stood with both arms out. He took back his left hand, changed his mind, and then put out his right. If you were driving past, you would have seen a man who looked foolish and possibly even a bit deranged. But up close, it was heavenly.

"Shake my *left* hand," said Stinker. "It's closer to my *heart*."

They shook.

Gwyneth's eyes drifted down to the stretch of material on the inside of Stinker's denimed thighs. She noticed they were bleached whiter than the rest of the jeans from him caressing his manhood. She wondered if this beast would be freaky in the feathers, a true "gash jockey."

Ridin' 'em bareback and fancy free . . .

Gwyneth felt her crotch grow warm to the touch. *It felt good to want a man again. This man who was all a dream, hominy grits and double cream . . .*

YATAG, she thought. *You are the angel glow.*

Stinker, too, was in love. He again felt like a 12-year-old with a crush on his gorgeous teacher who just happened to be in her mid-fifties, the one he'd have an illegal relationship with and then get kicked out of school forever because of.

But this woman who stood before him now—this incredibly rich, well-bred creature who had no business standing without a man by the side of I-95—took Stinker's arms in hers and marveled at their dirty downiness.

She never looked back. She didn't need to.

Chapter 9

PUMP IT!

Orville Max the III was immaculately dressed:
Perfectly-tailored black suit, black tie and black shoes.
Even the flower in his lapel was black.

The flower was a carnation, which symbolized cut-rate, mass-produced death that the women didn't particularly enjoy.

This was his uniform.

Everyone had one.

Orville Max sat within his downtown apartment, overlooking the great city of Atlanta below.

The Big A. The Big Peach. A-town. Hot 'Lanta.

The "West Hartford" of the South.

God, how this great city had changed! So much insanity and uncertainty. Not the way it used to be. Not the way it should *be.*

The apartment—all 5,000 square feet—was rigged out with all that was current and none that was dated: shag carpeting from floor to ceiling and then back over to floor, and then over to the front door, which was also shagged from top to bottom, and then back up to the ceiling, and then back over to the floor, stopping only at the avocado-green wi-fi cabinets, which extended over to the huge hot-goldenrod microwavable oven, leaking radiation every which way but loose.

Also, a rattan sex chair.

And an indoor cactus garden.

Fancy owl wallpaper, too.

And curtains that were controlled by remote control. *An urban Graceland.*

The goddamn place had cost Orville a virtual fortune, $35,000.

But it truly was a *beaut.*

Orville Max sat deep within his leather couch just below his framed military honors, and stared intently at a glossy photo of Stinker. Orville hated Stinker and his type. Takers. Scragglers. Hoodlums. The denim-flared. Sideburns down to the curlies. Yogurt practitioners. Unitarians. What else?

Those who swam at the Y.

Porn-store cashiers with an attitude.

He hated them all.

Oh . . . tourists who lamely attempted to eat slabs of marbled boardwalk fudge with plastic sporks . . .

Regardless, the weak- and knock-kneed were ruining this wonderful country with their levity and their light-heartedness. Their love for the Sunday funnies. Their disrespect for the law. Their permissiveness . . .

This country—this wonderful country that his grandparents from Germany had snuck into using false documents that hid a certain past—was no place for levity. Not with the Communists bearing their red-fanged choppers into all that was sacred and then ripping it all to shreds. Now was the time for *strength.* What was now needed was a mottled, arthritic, middle-aged hand, like the one belonging to the dear, departed President.

The great man had been run out of office by sissies.

And that was a *real* shame.

Orville had loved the man like a father. And the great man had loved Orville back like a son. No, he wasn't always a perfect father. He had his problems. In fact, he was a terrible, abusive father. Often, he was impatient. Sometimes he was curt. Violent. A bit oily. But he was a saint compared with that big-toothed goofball currently occupying the honorable office. A do-gooder. A wimpy weakling. A Lefty Lou.

A pansy *afwaid* of wabbits, for crying out loud!

Orville took out a "Semper Fi" rag and then his bottle of silicone lubricant. It was time to wipe down his shotgun. He'd do so with care. With precision. With a love and a respect that was no longer evident in this failing country. Smooth, long strokes. Nice and even jerks, with the lubricant making a soft sigh and a delicious slurp.

This was nice.

Orville pumped faster. And faster. And then even faster.

Suddenly he stopped, out of breath.

Pumped one more time for good measure.

Now, a little sleepy, he peered through the M-16 rifle's sites. "Bang," he muttered. "Bang, bang. Prepare to die! Stinker go bye bye!"

If the great man was still in power, he'd have agreed that Stinker had to go. And the great man would have helped.

But the great man was sadly no longer in power.

So, as it was—and probably always would be— Orville Max the III was entirely on his own.

Orville again began to pump.

He had more than enough anger jam to make it through the night.

Chapter 10

INTO THE WOODS WE GO, WE GO!

With great and loving care, Rascal was picking the numerous crumbs and nits out of Stinker's 'stache.

The entire gang—including the woman who still had no name—sat on a picnic blanket next to a gorgeous man-made lake built behind an office park off I-95.

The grassy spot sat just behind the area where the geese slept and frequently defecated.

Paradise.

"So," the woman said to Boner. "How did you and Stinker meet?"

"Well," said Boner. "*That's* a story you'll have to hear one day!"

"Go for it," said the woman. "All I have is time."

Boner smiled. *This girl is so very beautiful. If she didn't belong to my best friend, I would touch her like a doctor . . .*

"Well, see here," began Boner. "Have you ever heard of the Rainbow Reachers?"

"I don't think so," replied the woman.

"Some might call it a cult," said Boner. "For many years I called it home. Until I needed to escape. A friend of a friend told me about Stinker. Said in all humility that he was the greatest man in all of the universe. I didn't believe him. But I learned *real* quick."

"How?" asked the woman, inquisitively.

"He led me away from the clutches of Father in the middle of the night. A daring escape. Didn't even charge me. Only asked that I give up my career in the arts—I had devoted my life to sculpting driftwood pieces into the shapes of lesser-beloved Biblical characters. Told me that I'd now have to spend the rest of my life assisting him on his many amazing adventures."

"True?" the woman asked Stinker.

"As true as this here thigh mustache," Stinker replied, pointing 'tween his thighs.

Quickly changing the subject, the woman motioned to Rascal: "What a sweet girl! I just wanna *cuddle* her!"

"Wouldn't be so smart," said Jumbo, his muzzle shiny with fried-chicken juice. "This here monkey might appear all roses and apples but she's more bitter than a Georgia hen in a kosher deli."

"Ain't a monkey," mumbled Stinker. "She a *chimp*."

"Righto," said Boner. "She's got more zippity kick than Evel Knievel's American Eagle 750cc."

"Shithouse!" cried Buck. "Shithouse, shithouse, *shithouse*!"

Everyone laughed except for Gwyneth, who found it disturbing.

"You know," said Stinker, licking strange-yellow butter substitute off his fingers, "we never did find out your name. Care to tell us?"

The woman, who was eating all proper and dignified with the expensive cutlery she had brought along in her knock-off Gucci luggage, smiled daintily and replied: "Gwyneth. Gwyneth Lace. And it is a rightful pleasure to meet *all* of your acquaintances."

"What gives?" asked Jumbo, just before belching.

Boner struck Jumbo on the back of his head. *The damn fool had no manners in front of anyone . . .*

"What I meant," continued Jumbo, "is just how such a lovely Bambi ended up with such an ugly batch of badgers as us?" He belched again.

You could lead a fat pig to a bag of sorghum . . .

"Oh, I wouldn't say any of you are ugly now," said Gwyneth, her long hair catching a tint of the sun's late-afternoon rays. "In fact, you're just the anecdote I need from the poison I've been consuming."

"What type of poison?" asked Boner, growing serious. This girl was like nothing he'd ever witnessed. He was used to the more . . . gritty variety. The type with "sweet" tattooed on one breast, "sour" on the other. With silver-plated pirate earrings in areas where the sun don't shine. With genital warts where the sun *do* shine.

"Such as a society that looks down on all those who want to be *free*," explained Gwyneth.

It seemed like she had spent a very long time keeping this speech to herself, and it was now tumbling out quickly, almost in a torrent. "A society where you don't have to marry the stodgy, eldest son of mother's best friend. Where you can, instead, fall in love with a *real* man with cigar burns on his inner thighs." She glanced over to Stinker, who blushed.

He *never* blushed.

But this was different.

Oh, how this was different.

"Like a world in which you're told to do *this* and told to do *that*," said Gwyneth. "Where a rich girl with no job and no plans and 'mental issues' can run naked through the woods behind an elementary school at noon and not be arrested by a small-town police officer who knows only rules and not *possibilities*."

Miss Becky, she a mean, lean machine!

Stinker treatin' the ladies to a little Tender Lovin' Stink!

Rock band The Shag Reflex!

Emergency workers take a quiet moment to contemplate
the multiple murders and mayhem!

Thousands of foxxy fans cheer on their
honky hero as he bravely races giant freak Bongo!

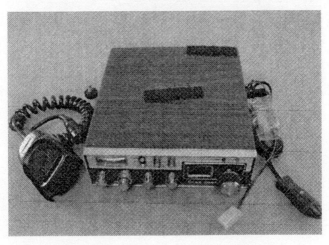

Communicatin' don't get no better than this!

At the lakeside picnic!

Boner ain't even got time for instant Sanka!

Pop 'er in, pull her out, pop 'er in, pull 'er out! *Niiiiice . . .*

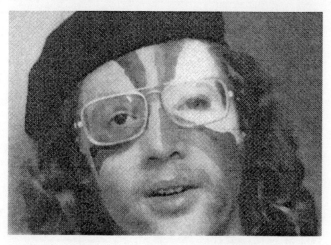

There's always ONE who don't get it!

Fat funnyman Jumbo is not allowed back in the state of Indiana!

"Got your ears on, good buddy? This here the Stinker!
Come back, come back!"

Stinker and Gwyneth make slinky outdoorsy love!

Mary Alice Tracy, Stinker's gorgeous 56-year-old teacher!

A "mooner" at nooner!

"You try to take away my bubble gum, I will teach you a lesson
you will *never* forget! Just joking!"

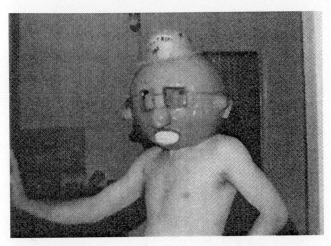

Bang Bang Billie entertains everyone with his wild antics!

"She may be an insane chimp but she's *my* insane chimp!"

Golden sunrise, fresh suds, 8-track cranking,
life don't get much better!

Gas shortage? Doc has *plenty* to go around!

Ain't nothin' finer than a Southern diner!

The hot-air balloon!

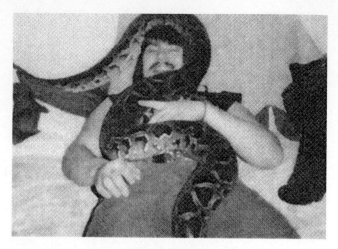

The rattlesnake!

The high-speed chase!

Stinker was blushing even harder.

It was time.

"Come with me," Stinker announced, standing. And then, looking down, he muttered: "*Whoops.*" He bent over, ashamed. This *never* happened outside the trailer. "Whoopsy daisy." His magoo was a-risin'.

Everyone laughed, except for Buck, who didn't quite understand. One day he might. Probably within a year or so. Maybe less. Eight months, tops.

"I think it's time you and me hit those dark, deep woods," said Stinker, pointing to the deep, dark woods adjacent to the lake. "Oh, I do indeed."

Dinky dunkin' in the woods. This was Stinker's sexual "thing." Everyone had one.

Gwyneth's "thing" was holding mewling, squiggly baby rats from failed strip-mall pet stores and wondering what they could ever be thinking.

Boner's was hugging amusement park mascots without their knowledge and permission long after security announced, "Step away, sir."

Jumbo's was sneaking into sausage factories and prancing about with stolen bouffant safety caps.

"Why, whatever do you mean?" asked Gwyneth to Stinker, feigning ignorance. She *knew.*

The sexual tension was delicious. Which wasn't a surprise. Gwyneth was a Gemini-Sagi. Stinker, a double Cancer. Together: kickapoo joy juice.

Gwyneth thought of Stinker naked against her now, his penis like a phallic thimble.

Stinker said nothing more. *Didn't need to.*

He pushed Gwyneth—gently but with manly determination—straight into Mother Nature's fragrant thicket.

Gwyneth could not resist.

How could any woman?

Chapter 11

OKIE DOKIE, BIG AND LIL' SMOKEYS!

The tiny man and his big smokey daddy sat in their camouflaged deer stand in the middle of the South Carolina woods, located just behind Doc's Fillin' Station, two hundred miles as the crow flies from where Stinker was now makin' slinky, outdoorsy love on top of a plastic garbage bag to create a barrier between his half nude body and pesky insects and twigs.

The tiny smokey held his miniature binoculars up to his baby-like eyes, while his father, head-to-toe in plaster cast, mumbled and complained.

"Daddy, I told you, I *will* get them," said the tiny man, annoyed by his father's frequent, incessant complaints.

Only his father's lips could move but he was certainly making the best of that! Every bone in the old man's body was broken. And *this* was what he was worried about? A beer-battered troubled troubadour by the name of Stinker?

The little man was small but he wasn't stupid. He had meticulously mapped out Stinker's trajectory and saw that the low-rent lothario was heading north. Saw that Stinker would run out of gas halfway between Atlanta and Charleston. Knew that all the *legal* gas stations between here and Portland, Maine would already be running low on fuel, and that lines would be long. There was only one place for Stinker to head.

Stinker didn't wait for gas.

Stinker didn't wait for *nothin'*.

The little man knew that when Stinker truly needed his Go-Go juice, he'd have to stop at this South Carolina swampy moonshine station, where *all* the degenerates had been filling up their mean machines since the towel heads had started hording God's precious black milk.

Plenty of motion potion to go around . . .

There was never a line. There was as much gas as one would ever need. You just had to know the right person. And for those who rode the highways and byways of this glorious nation—and did so for a living—the "right person" was a frizzed up, tweaked out, sizzled and grizzled backwoods skunk who smelled of bad soil and angry intentions.

His name was Doc and he'd been dealing diesel for as long as country phreaks had been hustling bootleg motor drink.

Doc lived in a tumbled-down sheetrock shebang way back yonder.

Good luck finding it.

Doc had earned his degree on the dirt trails, with a major in attitude and a minor in brashness. His B.S. degree would have read "Shim Shammery."

Seventy-five years old now, with a broken nose and a weak prostate.

Kicked out of the military for fragging a Yankee cook for mispronouncing "jambalaya."

But a strong mind.

And a liver that was showing signs of severe cirrhosis.

And an extra nipple, located on his lower back.

And yet, he was a good man.

And *dependable* . . . unlike the sheriff, who was now mumbling something incoherent. It came out like "*Mmph popa doddle treyf?*"

The little man rolled his little eyes and shook his tiny head. "No, daddy. Stinker don't arrive until later tonight. But we'll be ready."

"*Brahp dhmpa bump noodle?*"

"No, daddy. I don't know when. That's why I got us here so early."

The sheriff tried to nod, found that he couldn't, and went back to sucking on his frozen blueberry-flavored carbonated beverage. A blue stream slid down his chin and then onto his plaster full-body cast.

It was funny because the sheriff was encased entirely in white. And the drink was blue.

The little man dabbed the old man's face with his sleeve but then thought better of it.

He'd get to that later. Better to keep watch.

You never knew when a crazy-ass grinder such as Stinker might come burstin' on through . . .

You just never knew.

Chapter 12

STINKER DON'T REVERSE!

Stinker and Boner were in a hairy, wrinkled pickle.

It was a few hours after the picnic and Miss Becky was now roughly five miles South of the South Carolina border, on a dirt road, before a raging creek, with nowhere to go.

Stuck.

The bridge that spanned the two sides was nowhere to be found.

A sign read:

"MEN WORKING – DO NOT ATTEMPT TO JUMP!!! NO BRIDGE! *REALLY* DANGEROUS!"

Now see, this here was a problem.

Why?

Cause Stinker didn't reverse.

Never had, never would.

Never even thought to learn.

As capable as he was moving forward, Stinker was the complete *opposite* when it came to going backwards.

And he liked it that way.

But not everyone did.

Boner, for one.

"Got your ears on?" Boner barked into the CB mic

from inside his truck, just behind the Trans. "I say, got your ears on, Stinker?"

Boner's CB crackled and then there was the melodious voice of Stinker: "Big mound of turkey turd ahead, son. A plate of shit biscuits and squirrel gravy! But you know the rules: no reversin' or I'll be cursin'."

Next to Boner, Jumbo was now spreading fried-chicken fat on his belly and spelling his name upside down:

oqɯnſ

"Stinker, listen up and listen good," continued Boner. "We got a President to meet and a frosty shipment of hops to hand over. We ain't got zero time for no Stinker nonsense now!"

Boner paused to formulate the double negatives. He shrugged.

"Come back, come back!"

There was only silence. Boner realized it was useless to argue with the man. It was like arguing with a tree stump in a discount chainsaw store.

Boner's mic let out a screech and he knew that Stinker had turned off the transmitter on his end.

Can't stand the truth, is what.

Stinker mashed the mic's button three times. And waited.

Nothing.

Stubborn bastard, thought Stinker.

Got commodity butter in his ears. I'll meet him at Doc's. Let him find his own damn way. Besides, it'll take him half the shape-shiftin' night to jump that creek—if he don't kill himself first. God speed to idiots and honkey-heads who don't reverse . . .

"Where we headed?" asked Jumbo from Boner's passenger seat, finishing his bucket of chicken and starting on a steaming deep-dish pizza pie topped with very large crawdaddies.

At least he *hoped* they were crawdaddies.

"Away from this shit on a shingle," said Boner, putting the truck into a three-point turn, which was incredible—there was *very* little room.

The truck's clock read 4:45.

The three-point turn turned into a thirty-two point turn.

The truck's clock now read 4:46.

It was *incredible . . .*

"Enough of this jaw jackin'!" Boner announced. "Time to get this wiggle wagon a'-wangin'! Sometimes you just have to pay the water bill at the fandago factory and this is one of those times!"

Jumbo made a mental note to find out what this all meant later.

Boner launched into his spastic cartoon character that made everyone crack up whenever there was a tense situation: "I say, I say, I say *a-a-a-a-a-a-away* from here!"

Jumbo cheered and then made the universal sign for truckers to pull the air horn. Typically only children and adults with below-average intelligence made this request, but this did not stop Jumbo.

Boner drove away, horn blasting, with Rascal in the back.

Or at least he *thought* Rascal was in the back.

Chapter 13

WHY, AIN'T HE A ...

What goes on inside the mind of a wild chimp?

No one knows—not even the wild chimp experts.

Perhaps not even the chimps, themselves.

Rascal was no better or worse than any other wild chimp.

She was uncultivated and unruly and violent and horrible to be around, with breath that smelled worse than prolonged death.

Her fur was overripe and her eyes were a pulsating and deathly yellow. Her claws were violently sharp and her tail was half swollen with jungle rot.

But that's typical.

What wasn't typical was her need for freedom.

What goes on inside the mind of a wild chimp?

No one knows.

But perhaps it goes something like this:

Rascal need freedom.

Rascal lonely.

Rascal want jungle sex with male chimp.

Maybe or maybe not.

Something of that high-degree of scientificness can never be accurately established.

Knowing what animals thought was more an art than a science.

Just ask the scientists.

What *could* be determined was that Rascal had escaped from out of her circus chains in the back of the truck, and was now making her primate-like way through the woods to an undetermined location to participate in sexual congress, but not on top of a plastic garbage bag.

Rascal want it.

Rascal need it.

Now.

What goes through the mind of a wild chimp?

God only knows.

And maybe not even Him.

Especially not Him.

Chapter 14

RASCAL LETS LOOSE!

Orville Max the III saw the strangest thing.

If he was a swearing man—and he wasn't—Orville would have fucking sworn that he'd just seen a monkey break out from the back of the truck close to where he was now parked. Orville knew for certain that Stinker was not traveling alone—he seemed to have been joined by at least one female and one very fat pathetic excuse for a human—but was there also a *circus animal* with them?

Not that this animal was cute.

Far from it.

This creature seemed diseased with madness, like the rest of the country.

And yet there was a certain bloodshot, cross-eyed look in its heavy, unnaturally-lidded eyes that Orville could relate to.

A look of fear but also of unleashed power.

Sick of being held down by those who were weaker and stupider.

I won't kill this monkey, thought Orville. *I will not kill this monkey. He's like me. Berserk . . . but with a good soul. And a very large and inflamed rear-end.*

Orville sat in his 1977 Cadillac DeVille, an American car not limited in any way by Oriental cheapness. His car stereo system blasted opera, the only style of music that Orville could abide.

Specifically, Wagner.

True, Rick Wagner wasn't an American composer—he was East German—and yet his tunes spoke universal truths through soaring melodies and lovely crescendos. To Orville, Wagner seemed like the type of guy you could sidle up next to at a bar and just talk politics.

Although it wasn't a word Orville used often, Rick Wagner was "cool."

Orville watched the monkey gallop off through the woods, away from where the Trans Am sat. The animal seemed intent on leaving quickly. Orville wished it luck.

He had his own problems to worry about.

Namely . . . *how to take Stinker out?*

Speaking of which:

Why was Stinker's car just idling in place all this time? What was going on inside? And was it sexually related?

Orville grew excited and began to imagine what Wagner would think. Would he share a brewski with Orville and watch Stinker and his lady goin' at it, all hammer and tongs?

Or would Ricky be difficult and claim that it wasn't the "right" thing to do?

Orville had no idea.

He really didn't.

Life wasn't an opera.

Chapter 15

THE DAY'S CLOSE!

Within the labia-red naugahyde interior of Miss Becky, Gwyneth and Stinker were having their first fight.

If it wasn't so mean-spirited, it would have been adorable.

In the backseat, next to the priceless six-pack of Schlitz within an empty cardboard diaper box, Buck was fast asleep. He was dozing off a boozy afternoon.

"Now how would you know?" asked Stinker, with exasperation. "How could you *possibly* know the best angle in which to launch this here car over this here creek?"

Gwyneth just looked at him.

Stinker asked, "How would you know *anything* about cars? Or creeks?"

Gwyneth reached deep into her fancy knock-off Gucci purse and pulled out an oddly-shaped piece of plastic with numbers on it. Stinker's eyes narrowed and settled on a fecal point in the middle distance just as they always did when he was confused or having an orgasm.

"Huh?" he mumbled. "*Whaaaaa?*"

"I didn't want to tell you this earlier," proclaimed Gwyneth, "but I make my living as a mathematician. As a matter of fact, I am one of the best mathematicians in the entire world."

"Speak English," said Stinker. "In this country we speak *English*."

"This," said Gwyneth, holding up the disturbing piece of plastic, "is called a *protractor*. Do you know what mathematicians use protractors for?"

Stinker smiled. "When you love tractors, you're *pro*-tractor," declared Stinker, impishly. He blew a bubble, which smelled of wild apples.

"No," said Gwyneth, losing patience with this moronic yet enchanting Southern savage. Her neck was turning red, a sure sign of the temper that was so strongly linked to her Irish heritage. "A protractor is used to determine angles."

"Angels," repeated Stinker.

"No, *angles*," said Gwyneth. "What degree of angle we must launch this car in order to successfully land on the other side."

Stinker let out one of his signature laughs, which would have sounded obnoxious or off-putting if it came from anyone but from a man who owned a pet iguana named Harry Pussè who lived beneath a French fry lamp.

"The only pro . . ."

"Protractor," said Gwyneth, losing patience.

"The only *protractor* I ever need is right in *here*," Stinker said, pointing first down to his groin, and then back up to his head. "And this here protractor is saying that we need to jump at . . ."

He paused. And then spread his arms wide.

"*This* angle to make it. I've done it before. I intend to do it again. That's why I built the dirt ramp like that." He pointed to the dirt ramp that he had just built like that. Stinker's brain was the original "thinking machine."

"If we take that angle, we will most certainly die. Is that what you want?"

"Honey, I live by a different set of numbers and rules," Stinker said. "My numbers come from the streets. And the stars."

Gwyneth looked confused.

"Anyway," continued Stinker, with great confidence in his heavenly eyes, "we shall be fine. As sure as the day is long."

"Right," said Gwyneth.

"Just relax," said Stinker, but the confidence in his dazzling eyes was already beginning to fade. It could switch *that* fast. "Stinker don't reverse."

"I know," said Gwyneth, fed up. "So you've said. But I am extremely tired of even attempting to get anything through that thick, hairy head of yours. *Just go.*"

"Honey," said Stinker, "you're in the right hands." He made a fist. "Don't worry about a thing."

Exhaust poured from the Trans's triple-dual system, the only one of its type in all of Georgia.

"Ready?" asked Stinker, knowing full well that this was as ready as he'd ever be.

"As ready as I'll ever be," replied Gwyneth, knowing full well that this was as ready as she'd ever be. But what else could she do? It was too late in the game to change her mind. Her life was already in Stinker's freakishly veiny hands. And there wasn't a damn thing she could do about it.

She liked this feeling.

All women do.

Stinker popped Miss Becky into Drive—with *finesse*, just like she *wanted* it; no, *needed* it—and Miss Becky fishtailed her way down the dirt road, slowly at first . . .

10 mph.

20.

. . . and then with more speed.

30 mph.

40.

This wasn't good. If Stinker didn't reach 75 mph—preferably faster—they were all goners, including Miss Becky . . .

50 mph.

60.

65.

So close . . .

70 mph.

"C'mon, girl," said Stinker, stimulating her compliant dashboard with his ring finger. "Do it for your ol' man. C'mon, baby."

The vibration of the engine stirred an aching in Stinker's groin that had not been satisfied in hours.

"Not enough speed!" screamed Gwyneth over the roar of the one-of-a-kind V48 engine.

"Almost there," replied Stinker. "Scooch on over, girl. *Scooch!*"

"Not enough angle!" screamed Gwyneth.

"*Plenty* enough angle!" screamed Stinker. He usually didn't scream. Specially just after a woman did.

Bang!

The front windshield of Miss Becky exploded out

with a horrible explosion. Glass blasted back into the car, spraying both Stinker and Gwyneth and even Buck, who was still sleeping off the day's drink.

Even in his sleep, Buck was cursing.

It was adorable.

Somehow, Stinker managed to keep control . . . but noticed with great fear that he had only hit the dirt ramp at 72 mph.

Would it be enough?

Stinker had to admit he didn't think it would be.

He also had to admit that he had made up the 75 mph fact. Maybe it was 85. Or even 100. *Was this really happening?*

Stinker took another sip of giggle water.

He sometimes called it Colorado Kool-Aid.

To other people who weren't in "the life," it was simply called "beer."

Stinker's head hurt.

Or was it his neck?

Stinker didn't know.

Too many goddamn questions.

Stinker closed his eyes and experienced perhaps his last-ever thought:

He was riding a stolen donkey ass-back and fancy free in the parking lot of a rendering plant while humming "Goober Peas" and pleasuring himself with a shoplifted bottle of Body on Tap. It was a thought most great men have before dying.

Stinker closed his eyes and bravely hoped for the best.

Chapter 16

BANG BANG!

"Will it be enough to get over the creek?" Orville had asked himself a few moments earlier. "Not a chance. But why take a chance?"

Orville pulled out his military-issued M-16 rifle and aimed for Stinker's Trans Am's front windshield.

"Semper Fi," said Orville, as he pulled off a shot.

It missed.

At that moment, Orville could almost smell Saigon. The whores. The dope. The pimps. The saffron. The back-gutter wrench of a country turning from good to bad, from safe to miserable.

Also, elephant dung.

Lord, the elephant dung. Orville remembered a time when all he could smell was the fumy excreta of those great, loping beasts.

In all honesty, he missed it.

Horribly.

Orville quickly took one last shot, all ricky-tick.

Bookoo dinky doo.

The front window of Miss Becky caved in on itself, glass flying inward.

The explosion was tremendous.

"Stinker go *au revoir*," declared Orville. "Bang bang! And boo hoo!"

In his mind's eye, Orville saw an elephant smile.

Those damn beasts.

Jungle shitters never forgot.

Chapter 17

UH OH!

It *wouldn't* be enough.

Stinker knew this now, and he was so very sorry he had ever attempted such a stupid stunt. *What was he thinking?* His brain was fuzzy from beer. He had consumed two since hitting the dirt ramp.

"We are going to die!!!!" screamed Gwyneth.

Like most elegant ladies of her upper-crust ilk, she despised using contractions.

"Yes," said Stinker, all calm. Over the years, whenever thinking about dying, he had imagined he'd do so in a puddle of urine, not his own.

How wrong he had been!

"Yes, we are gonna die," Stinker declared. "So . . . penny for your thoughts?"

"How about a nickel?" asked Gwyneth.

Even when dying she could be wonderfully quippy.

"Only got a penny," replied Stinker, who could also be just as quippy. "But it's a shiny one!"

The smell of his own fear blasted through his nostrils. Stinker gagged.

Miss Becky was flying over the creek but it was not nearly fast or high enough.

Stinker took Gwyneth's hand in his and held both up high. If someone had been standing on shore, they would have seen a convertible Trans Am soaring through the air, but just about to crash, with a driver and his passenger holding hands. It was a beautiful sight. Alarming but beautiful.

Stinker was well aware of the blown-out front windshield but he would worry about that some other time. Either way, he was a winner.

"Goodbye, baby," Stinker said to Gwyneth. "I always did love you."

"And me, you," said Gwyneth, in that elegant way of hers. She had never seen herself dying while jumping over a sad, little-known Georgia creek in a leased Trans Am, but there were far worse ways to go. She couldn't think of any at the moment, but she'd think about all this later. Or not at all.

Either way, she, too, was a winner.

Buck, blissfully unaware of what was happening, continued to snooze away the day, surrounded by broken glass. The kid was *really* passed out.

Stinker would have to remember to give Buck less Cajun napalm the next time the kid was in need of mental escape from his horrible, relentless mountain thoughts.

Gwyneth and Stinker prepared to enter a new realm of consciousness. Wherever the two ended up—even hell itself—the kid and Miss Becky would just have to follow.

Chapter 18

COULD THIS BE?

Orville almost wished he could somehow film this amazing scene, much like a director would with a big budget Hollywood movie that supposedly took place down South but was really shot in California and that showed for a few nights at a handful of Southern theaters and drive-ins before closing forever.

Orville hoped time would slow down so that he'd be able to experience all of this in slow motion.

Stinker was going to die. And Orville had had a hand in it.

When he was in-country, Orville had killed many gooks—perhaps up to a few hundred—and had not shed one precious American tear over any of them. Well, there was that one he had cried about, but she was a spy and Orville hadn't cried for long—maybe thirty seconds. Just long enough to wash away that womanly smell, get back into his uniform, polish his boots, and proceed on with his day, including wrestling nude with his well-oiled (olive, military grade) best pal, Buzzy. In retrospect, the female gook probably wasn't a spy after all. Just a female with more intelligence than she needed for her own damned good.

Maybe she wasn't even a gook.

Or a female.

But this kill felt different.

Orville was grinning wide. It almost hurt. *Muscles not used to this,* he thought. *Haven't been this happy since the "Saturday Night massacre." Or at least that's what the Jew press had called it. Best night of my life.*

The Trans Am was still flying through the thick Southern air, but with its front windshield blown to bits, she was dropping.

And quickly.

Not a chance she'll make it over, thought Orville.

But Orville's grin quickly turned into a grimace.

Can't be, he thought. *How could this possibly be? Stinker was as good as dead! What is happening here?!*

What was happening was that the Trans was going to make it, after all.

This could be an opera . . . I swear to my Lord, this could be a goddamn opera! thought Orville. *Not one of those horrible rock operas about a lippy, hippy, goateed Jesus who looked as if he worked at a scented-candle store. But an opera with a fat dyke singing in a grating East German tongue.*

The only kind worth listening to.

Orville was locked and loaded, the safety long off.

Full-metal banquet.

Jack it!

With the opera blaring and an imaginary Rick Wagner sucking on his love knuckle—the guy really *was* cool—Orville watched the resurrection of this man they called "the Stinker."

If it wasn't so horrifying, it would have been beautiful.

Maybe life *was* an opera, after all.

Chapter 19

NICE LANDING!

Stinker had already prepped for the end. He was ready for whatever was about to come his way. His only regret in life was that he should have done more aimless driving and transporting of very low-grade hop-infused substandard stagger juice for very little cash, but that's a wish all men have.

Stinker was at peace.

Gripping Gwyneth's hand even tighter, Stinker waited for the all-encompassing darkness to envelop them both. *It might even be relaxing,* thought Stinker. *Finally take that long-awaited vacation everyone's been begging me to take.*

I just work too damn hard doin' nothin'...

But instead of darkness, there only came more sunshine.

And Stinker felt life.

Looks like that much-needed rest might just have to wait 'til I do a whole lot more nothin'...

Stinker grinned. And mentally hugged himself.

He couldn't help himself.

He was adorable. And the self-hug felt *good.*

In the meantime, Miss Becky landed with a gentle thud on a hard surface.

"What in the deviled-hammed creation?" asked Stinker, mostly to himself. But if anyone else heard what he had just said, then that was okay, too.

He had made it up. And he was proud.

"Are we in heaven?" asked Gwyneth.

"We ain't in hell," chimed Stinker, grabbing hold of the wheel and coming to a quick break.

But where exactly were they?

"Fuck?" asked Buck, from the backseat. He had just woken up, breath reeking of razzleberry wine. "Wop?"

Carefully, Stinker looked out his driver's side window. The car looked to have landed on steel.

Could it possibly be . . . yes, it most definitely could be!

Stinker had landed *on top* of Boner's truck!

"Are we alive?" asked Gwyneth.

Her eyes were still tightly closed.

"More than alive," said Stinker. "Not dead, girl!"

"Not dead," mumbled Gwyneth. "Oh, thank god!"

"Just thank me," said Stinker. "I *told* you that angle was correct! Not even close."

Gwyneth opened her eyes. She shot Stinker a look that might as well have said, *You are truly something! But I love you anyway! I cannot help myself! No woman possibly could . . . even if you aren't in good shape and have a visible vasectomy scar . . .*

Carefully—ever so carefully—Stinker stepped from out of his car. He had less than one foot to maneuver.

Stinker had *stuck* the landing. *No surprise.*

Stinker yelled down to Boner: "Not bad, huh?"

Boner yelled back, "Couldn't leave you hanging, hoss! I took the long way 'round and then backed straight into the creek. Shortened your distance! Unlike you, I *do* reverse!"

"Owe you, buddy!" asserted Stinker.

"Just a few cans of suds," responded Boner, already drinking one down to celebrate.

Down in the truck's cab, Boner turned to Jumbo, who had spilled half the crawdaddy pizza onto his loamy, burbling lap.

Boner started to laugh. And Jumbo soon joined in.

Above, Stinker also began to laugh. And then Gwyneth, as well.

The mirth was infectious.

Buck, too, laughed. But for a far different reason. No one knew why.

"What are you doing with the rest of your life?" asked Stinker, winking.

Gwyneth tried to return the wink but found that she couldn't. She had a shard of glass in her left eye.

It was excruciating.

The gang was back together

And it felt *wonderful*.

Chapter 20

WHERE DAT FAT OL' SUN NE'ER DO RISE!

Stinker and Gwyneth and Buck crossed into South Carolina . . . still on top of Boner's truck. They were receiving some funny looks, mostly from the female variety. There were thumbs-ups from foxxy teen hitchers with hand-scrawled signs written in eyebrow pencil, and there were thumbs ups and okay signs and victory signs and finger shots and enthusiastic "stick-it-to-ems" and even one exceedingly elderly man—he looked to be at least 90—who gave them "the moon."

They could have done without seeing that . . . even beyond the colostomy bag.

Stinker was eased way back into his seat—all casual like—enjoying the last of the day's golden rays, baby-panda-leather cowboy boots up on Miss Becky's fleshy dash.

Miss Becky didn't seem to mind.

It was a damn good thing to have ended up on the top of Boner's truck. Miss Becky was out of gas and they were now only loaded with "sailboat fuel"—running on empty.

Soon, though, they'd be pulling into Doc's for a quick fill-er-up and then they'd be on their way to Chocolate City to meet Mister Numero Uno. Stinker would get back to drivin' a Trans that was all full of spunk and funk.

The entire gang would arrive with plenty of time to spare and just enough time to tear it up . . . yup!

Everything was coming up camellias.

Easy as a dollop of 'nilla on a steamin' slice of Ma's pie . . .

The truck pulled into Doc's backwoods filling station just as the strong Southern sun was setting. The colors reminded Boner of those found on the good ol' Reb flag. Also, a thigh bruise that never quite healed.

But it wasn't until Doc had taken Miss Becky down by crane and everyone was gathered around the moonshine refreshment distillery for a little late-afternoon night cap, that Buck pointed to the open doors at the rear of the truck and then ran back to where Stinker was sipping his 'shine.

The kid was a-hootin' and a-hollerin'.

"Fuck!" Buck said, pointing. "Fuck! Fuck! Fuck! FUCK!"

There was just something about the way that Buck had screamed that last "fuck" that sent chills down Stinker's manly spine. This was a different sort of "fuck" than Stinker was used to from this Appalachian imbecile. This one foretold of great danger. This was one disturbing "fuck."

"S'matter, boy?" asked Stinker, approaching warily. "Lost what's left of your square marbles?"

Boner was standing open-mouthed before the empty trailer. "Stinker, believe it or not, the idiot child's got a point," he said. "There's somethin' you need to see. Or *not* see."

"What's the matter, Bones?" asked Stinker, using Boner's nickname. Very few people ever used this nickname besides Stinker . . . and that 15-year-old bagger at Piggly Wiggly's back in Arkansas with the very small hips and the very hairy nips. But that was about it.

Boner spurted, "Your chimp done gone and escaped!"

"She *what*?!" yelled Stinker, peering inside.

Nothing.

Just circus chains and a large steaming mound of jungle pooty.

"Where in the hell did she go?" Stinker asked. "Goddamnit, son! Can't you carry nothin' 'cross state lines without *losing* it?"

"Now just a kitty-puckin' minute!" replied Boner. "Ease on down the road, boy, or your mustache gonna end up on the *back* of your head!"

"Relax!" exclaimed Gwyneth. "Relax, Stink! Relax, Bones!" This was her first time using Boner and Stinker's nicknames, and it felt *right*.

"What is important here is not who is at fault, but where we might be able to find poor Rascal!"

She still hated using contractions.

"Woman's got a point," said Stinker, suddenly looking cordite. "Let's focus our attention on finding the ol' girl." He paused. "Damnit to hell's back acre! And just when we were making record time, too!"

"Worms in a peach basket!" continued Jumbo.

For once, the jiggly-giggly fat man wasn't laughing or even trying to entertain. He looked to be genuinely concerned about the disappearance of this not-so-friendly chimp.

Jumbo's edible food stains had now spread down to his white socks.

He smelled terribly of sadness and public disgrace.

Stinker was beginning to regret ever having invited this swollen piece of garbage along for the ride.

All three stood before the back of the empty truck. Now what?

Things couldn't get worse.

But they *did*.

And *fast*.

From out of the bushes surrounding Boner's truck stepped forth a little man in petite boots and a miniature cowboy hat.

Stinker let loose with one of his signature high-pitched giggles. "Why, if it ain't the midget ankle-biter with a regular-sized attitude!"

"The knee-high shit-kicker, that's what ya called me!" replied the little man, pulling out a regular-sized gun. "So bite on *this*!"

The little man pointed his pistol directly at Stinker. His little forefinger went to pull the trigger. Gwyneth screamed. Her previous life had never allowed for midgets in tiny cowboy costumes using regular-sized guns. Her high-class urbane world had never known of such real-world circumstances.

In a way, she was a "road virgin."

And her "road cherry" was now being "popped."

It "hurt."

Stinker again prepared himself for his maker. He was getting good at this and he once again found himself at peace. He still had speckles of glass and a thin strand of bubblegum deeply entrenched in his dense 'stache. He was ready. But if the good trucker living in the big clouds above couldn't accept him just as he was—complete with a match head embedded in his secondary sex characteristics—well, then, maybe the good trucker shouldn't accept him *at all*.

Take me, Lord, Stinker thought. *Just provide me with enough cold beer for the long and lonely nights . . . that's all I ask . . . is that too much?*

Stinker grinned. He couldn't help himself. He dug "bending the ear" of the man upstairs.

Stinker then tensed for the bullet—which never arrived.

Instead, Stinker heard a horrible, high-pitched yelp.

Opening his eyes, Stinker saw that the little man was being attacked by none other than . . .

Rascal!

Who had returned!

It was so clear now!

When Rascal had escaped earlier from the truck, she had proceeded to get into many unbelievable adventures . . . only to return when she was needed most!

If Rascal talked, she would have told Stinker all about these phenomenal adventures.

But she couldn't. Which was good. Like most females, she probably never would have shut the hell up.

Chapter 21

RASCAL'S ADVENTURES!

Some of those adventures included:

Rascal meeting a blind woman who had allowed the chimp a long lick of her ice cream cone, thinking that Rascal was a handsome man with very bad breath who had just asked for her hand in marriage. The woman had wept and said "yes."

Rascal climbing aboard a hot-air balloon and waving to the children below and the children seeking shelter as Rascal went "wee wee."

Rascal riding through the streets of a small-town military parade, wearing medals, and taking full credit for the victory at the Battle of Normandy.

Rascal murdering a red-haired drifter by the name of Seahorse. No particular reason.

In short, Rascal was having the time of her chimp life, but she could still sense something amiss.

It was in the air. She could smell it.

Trouble.

And Rascal knew that she just had to help.

True, this distempered creature fallen from god's heavenly kingdom was in serious sexual heat and she desperately wanted—no, *needed*—to rut with a male chimp and it didn't matter *what* he looked like.

But this could wait. Stinker meant the world to her. And he needed her protection.

Rascal knew this instinctively . . . way down deep in her primal soul.

What goes through the mind of a wild chimp?

Maybe it was just as simple as saving your best pal from a midget with a gun.

So Rascal had waved to her fans, jumped from the balloon, breaking her fall on an already injured and now dead World War II veteran, and then made her way—with her incredible sense of scent (and a ride with a driver who had very little choice)—to this illegal backwoods distillery deep in the South Carolina woods.

And the feral chimp girl had arrived just in time.

Just.

Chapter 22

JUST IN TIME!

And here Rascal was now, doing her thing.

Stinker sat on a log. He knew very well what was about to happen and he wanted a good seat for it.

It was sure to be one hell of a show.

Damn chimp loves me, thought Stinker. *Just like every female out there, human or not . . .*

Boner, Gwyneth, Jumbo and Buck soon joined Stinker, taking seats on adjacent logs.

"Oh, I do love me some fighting," said Boner, all high-falutin', as if he was some sort of gay sports writer at an expensive, slick New York liberal weekly. "Oh I do! I do! I *reeeeaaaaallllllllly* do!"

Everyone laughed.

Even Doc—that ill-tempered piece of Dixie carcinogenic gristle—took one arthritic knee to the muddy patch to watch.

This was what was called good ol' backwoods entertainment.

Putting the whammy on sammy.

Stinker only wished that he had himself some buttered porn-theater popcorn to go with all the fun.

What goes through the mind of a wild chimp? Stinker thought.

Who the hell knows?

Then again, who the hell cares?

Kill 'em, girl.

Just kill the tiny freak!

The fight began.

Chapter 23

ALMOST THERE!

The fight was over.

It hadn't lasted long.

It had started slow but then increased in ferocity as Rascal found her sea legs. The sheriff and the tiny man had stood zero chance.

By the end, Boner had thrown in the towel, pretending to be a crusty boxing corner-man who had devoted his life to a love of stupendous and unnecessary violence both inside—and outside—the ring.

The "towel" was a stained jockstrap.

"You a tomato!" Boner screamed. "And ya too weak to fight a cold!"

Everyone laughed. It was too funny.

After the fight was mercifully over, Doc had scooped up both the sheriff and his freakish son—both barely alive—and placed them onto the bed of his Chevy pick-up's cab. He drove them straight off his property and arrived twenty minutes later by the side of a back road. He wrapped the tiny man head-to-toe in a plaster cast just as his daddy was already wrapped, and then propped both unceremoniously by the side of the road.

Best of luck to 'em.

It was now an hour later.

Jumbo was riding shotgun in Miss Becky. The front windshield was still blown out, allowing for the cool, refreshing Southern air to filter in.

Rascal was safely chained into the back of Boner's truck, daydreaming about all of her adventures. And yet she still seemed antsy. Perhaps she shouldn't have torn out the heart of that elderly World War II hero?

Buck was the front passenger in Boner's truck.

Boner was attempting to teach the kid some manners and wasn't have an easy time of it.

"Fuck," said Buck.

"*Love*," said Boner. "Say 'love,' boy."

"Fuck," said Buck.

"Love," said Boner. "It's all about love, brother. A long-haired trucker spoke about love hundreds of years ago. His name was Jesus. He didn't drive no truck but he *should* have driven one. He was a real good man and if he was still around, he'd wrap you up in his big ol' biblical shawl and hug you forever and ever and ever! And it'd be the best feeling in the entire world."

Boner paused.

"Well, the *second* best," Boner said. "After getting drunk."

"Shit," said Buck.

Boner rolled his eyes.

This mountain 'tard was impossible!

Within the cozy confines of Miss Becky, things were going much better.

Jumbo was doing his best imitation of a drunk whale. No one knew why. But no one was arguing.

"Now how did I get this dark ring of chocolate 'round my blowhole?" Jumbo asked, sounding for all the world *exactly* like an obese ocean critter.

Stinker and Gwyneth were laughing so hard tears were coming out of their eyes. It was a riot!

But Jumbo wasn't finished. He was just getting started.

"I juss a big ol' fat whale who like to go toot toot *toot*! Me *hungry*!"

Stinker was screaming with laughter and Gwyneth was rocking back and forth in shoulder-shaking hysterics.

This was the most uproarious thing they had *ever* witnessed!

They were having the time of their *lives*!

A truck passed on their left. The driver, a bearded road-brother with an American flag bandanna, waved.

Stinker knew this shaggy, long-haulin' fool from previous wanderings and was only too happy to see him again.

'Twas Jackass Jonnie.

Or Silverweed.

Or Elegant Bob.

No, Nasty Sam.

Willie the Wall-Eyed?

Yes. Definitely Nasty Sam.

One of 'em.

Whoever he was, Stinker would see him again down the road soon enough.

Amazing adventures were *never* in short supply.

Within five hours—plus or minus a few—Stinker would be handing off a nicely chilled six-pack of Schlitz to the President of the United States.

He was almost there.

Stinker flicked on his Panasonic RH-60 8-track player to take in some down-home country tuneage. A song blared out, smoky spicy and murky loud. It was the tune about Stinker:

Stinker, that good ol' boy, he never give up,
He do love everyone, whether they low or way, way up,
Stinker, that brawny, brave redneck,
he just won't never give up,
That powerful, powerful ol' man strong as ceeeee-ment.

The last word was off-putting as it didn't quite rhyme with what came before. The melody was discordant. It wasn't a great song—or even average . . . or even true, as it still didn't make much sense—but Stinker was okay with it.

He always was.

He turned it up even louder.

Chapter 24

CARAVAN!

Stinker wasn't sure how the word had started to spread . . . but it had. Must have been Nasty Sam.

Or Jackass Jonnie.

Or the Cocaine Kid.

Or Elegant Bob.

No. Definitely Nasty Sam.

Now *there* was a man who acted like a woman when it came to CB gossip!

The crowds had started small but as Stinker and the gang cruised their way north the throngs had grown larger and larger. In Rowland, North Carolina, just across the state line, Stinker drove beneath a bridge that had been decorated with flowers and hand-written signs. One sign looked to have been written by an elementary school group:

WE HEART STINKEя!

The R was backwards, signifying a deep, innocent love. But if the class had been just one year older, it would have been evidence of a profound stupidity.

For a guy who was kicked out of elementary school for having backseat sex with a teacher in her mid-fifties, Stinker was doin' a-okay for himself.

The mass of media had started to arrive just South of Fayetteville, with trucks, satellites and earnest-looking, college-educated reporters impotently holding up their expensive mics as Stinker drove past.

Stinker had no time for the government-run FCC.

Instead, he picked up his CB mic and went straight to channel 69:

"Nasty Sam, Nasty Sam. I'm talkin' to you now. Are you the one responsible for all this Stinker love?"

There was at first static and then a curt reply:

"Come back, come back. This here the Nasty Man. Let's say I did. Now what?"

Stinker smiled. In truth, he didn't mind becoming a celebrity. The country desperately needed someone to look up to in these dark, recession-drenched times. Why *not* him?

"Not mad at ya, Nasty," said Stinker into the gold-plated CB handset. "Just askin'. How ya find out where I was headed?"

"Huckleberry named Doc," said Nasty Sam. "Just enjoy the attention, son. All the way up to that goddamn swamp they call Washington!"

Washington came out sounding like *War-Shington*.

"That's a 10-4, good buddy," said Stinker. "Mercy sakes! Banana on the upswing, bang it and slang it! Crinkle and wrinkle! Slap and crap, stink and fink!"

Often, Stinker would like to make up his own CB slang, and this was one of those times.

Stinker turned to Gwyneth. "Ever think you'd be road famous?" he asked.

Gwyneth had to admit that she hadn't. A long time ago, as just a child and then as a teen, she had pictured herself as a world-famous math expert, married with two children, living the typical northeastern suburban boring dream. Had she ever envisioned delivering a six-pack of Schlitz to the President of the United States in a leased convertible Trans Am, joined by a near-mute holler hillbilly, an unhinged chimp, an amusing but smelly Southern fat man, and a trucker with an orgiastic sleeper cab who went by his god-given Christian name of Boner?

Never.

Jumbo was screaming:

"The Dallas Cowboy cheerleaders! The Dallas Cowboy cheerleaders!"

At first, Stinker thought the thick clown was hallucinating from one too many chocolate enemas, as was his habit—but not this time.

Stinker could now see the beautiful ladies, all in a row, as the Trans breezed past: the cheerleaders kicking their tasty legs and shaking their navy, silver and white pom-poms. The Dallas Cowboys were America's team. And the team's cheerleaders were America's lovelies. What they were doing in North Carolina, by the side of the road, was a bit of a mystery, but Stinker wasn't complainin'.

Meanwhile, Gwyneth imagined that she saw a black

person in the crowd but relaxed when it quickly became clear that this was only a fleeting apparition.

As Miss Becky headed north, the crowds grew more and more dense. When the car reached the North Carolina and Virginia border, the crowds exploded to eight deep. By Richmond, fifteen. By Charlottesville, twenty people stood behind every thirty who were already standing behind every forty alongside the road.

The nation had never seen anything like this.

Ever.

"Few more hours," said Stinker, out loud. "And our mission will be *finito*." It was the one word of Mexican he knew.

"Not so fast," said Gwyneth, pointing to a huge neon sign above the road.

Stinker groaned.

It read:

BIG RED CIRCUS IN 3 MILES!

"You told me earlier that you stole Rascal from a circus," said Gwyneth, coquettishly. "Might it be this one?"

"Well . . ." said Stinker. "I . . . don't remember."

"Sure you do," said Gwyneth. "This here is the circus. And if you found Stinker at this circus, perhaps we could also find her a mate . . ."

"Don't got the time, little lady," said Stinker. "I know what you're thinking, baby. But we just don't got the time! *Too close!*"

"Oh, we *always* have the time," said Gwyneth. "For love."

Stinker pointed to the back, where Jumbo was now asleep, his head on a six-pack pillow. Jumbo was snoring. In his sleep, he was mumbling about fast food restaurants, using very specific names, almost as if he was earning money by doing so.

With a pathetic air of male desperation, Stinker begged: "But, girl, we still got that precious brew to hand off!"

Gwyneth said nothing, just looked at Stinker.

Was she going to cry? Actually going to cry?

Stinker was done for. She started to cry.

"Goddarn it!" exclaimed Stinker, looking to the heavens above. "I'm talking money, woman! Good ol' American cabbage!"

Maybe she's going through that "change," thought Stinker sadly. *When does that happen again?* He thought back on his first teacher crush and her horrible, violent mood swings. Like most aging females, the teacher had definitely went and gone 'round that molasses twist.

"And I'm talking *love*," countered Gwyneth, between tears. "Only one thing that can tame that beast, and that's *love*. She is in *deep* heat."

Gwyneth was blubbering like a child. She had that look all women get when they become inflexible and impossible to deal with. Stinker had seen it before. Many times. And he knew it was useless to ever attempt to fight it.

Stinker sighed. Another battle lost.

"*One hour.* That's all. If she don't find a chimp man in that time, we head out regardless."

"Promise?"

"Promise," said Stinker.

"Pinkie promise?" chirped Gwyneth. Her voice was adorably high-pitched, like a vulnerable newborn's.

"Oh, c'mon now," extorted Stinker. "You know Stinker never, *ever*—"

"Stinker *will*," said Gwyneth, "or Gwyneth *won't*. If you know what Gwyneth *means*."

Stinker knew.

With his hand extended, Stinker promised.

"Are you missing a pinkie?" Gwyneth asked, shocked and a bit frightened.

Stinker blushed.

Then took the next exit.

Chapter 25

TAKING OFF!

Somewhere between Georgia and Washington D.C, Clarence MacLeod sat on his leather throne, within his office, on the top floor of the tallest building South of the Mason Dixon. Or "Masey Dixie" as Clarence's niece impishly called it. She wasn't bright.

Clarence was watching the latest satellite news coverage from around the country on his brand-new 85-inch, black and white, deep-set television. He had read about it in *Popular Mechanics* and knew immediately that he had to own it. It was the biggest in the world. Clarence adored it.

All the news for the past few hours had been about Stinker. Even Walter Cronkite had gotten into the act, hosting a "SPECIAL STINKER REPORT."

Every network in the country—all three of them—carried a live feed of Miss Becky making her way up the coast.

How much was Clarence paying Orville, again? $5,000? $7,000?

A whole damn lot.

And *this* was the result?

Clarence pressed the large red button on his desk. A dial tone could be heard. And then a woman's sexy, blonde-infused voice: "Yes?"

"Honey, it's Clarence. Get in here please."

"Yes, Mr. Clarence," replied the sun-dappled voice. "Right away, sir!"

Clarence leaned back in his leather chair and waited for the show.

Three, two, one . . .

In walked Betty, strutting and sashaying. She was a consistent gal, this Betty. Had been ever since that day Clarence had hired her for her . . . brains.

Good Lord, Clarence thought. *Now that's one gorgeous piece of a—*

"Assignment," asked Betty, taking a seat, cleavage packed all comfy-coo like two shoplifted Kash n Karry pimento loafs. "New assignment?"

Clarence pointed to his large television. "I've been watching the news, darlin'. And it's all about the Stinker."

"Oh yeah?" said Betty. A smile came to her face. She remembered what it had been like to sleep with Stinker. Like a broken carnival ride with no end.

"Oh yeah, oh *yeah*," said Clarence, in a mocking tone. "See, I had more faith in Orville's ability."

"Me, too," said Betty, half listening.

"Have we talked recently with our good friend Orville?"

Betty shook her head. Her fleshy cans wobbled like twin mounds of cake batter in a dollar-store mold.

Clarence stood: "Get in touch. Anyhow. *Anywhere.* And raise the price. To $60,000."

Betty gasped. "$*60,000*?!" She could barely get it

out. "D-d-d-d-do you think that's a good idea, Mr. Clarence?"

"Hell if I know," replied Clarence. "Orville's probably suffering from yellow-fever flashbacks. Running through the woods screaming about the gooks and sleeping with imaginary gays." He paused. "Which is acceptable. Heroic, even. But I *cannot* allow Stinker to reach the President and hand him Schlitz beer. And I'm running out of options here."

Clarence couldn't believe what he was about to say. But he said it anyway:

"Let's go with $75,000."

Betty let out a small scream. "That's . . . that's a tremendous alot!" she burbled, her breasts nodding in perfect agreement.

At least *they* weren't stupid.

Would this woman ever shut up?! thought Clarence. *If this woman happened to be a town, she'd be the main "drag."*

Clarence took the television remote and aimed it at Betty. He clicked the OFF button. It seemed to work.

Betty turned and exited the office. Clarence watched closely. He loved this free show, always did—nearly as much as watching anything on that gigantic black and white miracle of a modern-day appliance.

Almost.

As always, the girl didn't disappoint . . .

Chapter 26

IT'S ON!

The gang stood before the Indian owner of the Big Red circus.

The primitive's name was Big Red.

Gwyneth didn't think Big Red looked all that much like an Indian. To Gwyneth, Big Red looked Caucasian, perhaps even Canadian, but she wasn't about to ask questions. Not when standing in front of someone so important.

And *wise*.

"Now, Big Red," Stinker was saying, sucking on a piece of straw he had found over at the petting zoo area. "I'm not sure you know my history, but I do have a name."

"Big Red aware," said Big Red. "Man who drive in crazy way. Go by Stinker."

Stinker spit out the piece of straw he was chewing. It tasted very bad.

"First of all, I do want to apologize for taking Rascal a few months back," announced Stinker, wiping his mouth with the back of his hand. "But she's proved to be a most loyal friend."

"That so?" asked Big Red.

Everything the Indian uttered was sacred.

"But as you know from being around jungle creatures your entire life in the woods, even chimps need to find love."

Stinker was nauseated. Would this taste ever leave his mouth? He didn't think so.

"That so?" declared Big Red.

"That so," said Stinker. "I returned so I could find Rascal a most suitable partner. Of the chimp variety."

"Big Red understand," said Big Red.

Like most Indians, this fella wasn't the chatty type. Stinker knew this from watching a lot of television.

Half-breed was on a real Geronimo trip . . .

"Under one condition," continued Big Red.

"One condition?" asked Stinker, growing concerned. He thought this would be a cake walk. But with Indians, everything was *always* a mystery. Did they even like cake?

"That you win dirt road race against Bongo," said Big Red, adjusting his tremendously large Indian headdress, which seemed to be slipping a tad. It didn't appear to fit or contain real feathers. It also had a chin strap.

"Who in the hell is Bongo?" asked Stinker, now spitting out a petting-zoo feeding pellet and gagging.

"*That* Bongo," said Big Red, pointing.

Everyone looked over to a man—*was it even a man?!*—standing about fifteen yards away. They all turned at exactly the same time, which was very funny.

Then everyone took a step back, as if in shock, *also* at exactly the same time, which was *twice* as funny.

"That . . . Bongo?" asked Stinker, weakly.

"That *Bongo*," affirmed Big Red.

Bongo said nothing. He stood at least six feet tall. He was very muscular. He was not wearing a shirt.

His arms were huge, as was his stomach. Across his left cheek was a ragged scar. He was bald. He barely looked human. Was there a meaner man in the world?

"If you lose," said Big Red, emphasizing his words with his multi-colored plastic tomahawk, "you lose Rascal. And Rascal never find mate for loving."

Jumbo stepped forward. "Now that's not fair—"

Boner held him back, which wasn't easy. "Easy, fat man."

"I'm fine, Bones," said Jumbo, calming down.

"But if I do win . . . then what?" asked Stinker.

Big Red stretched his arms out wide to conjure the entire universe.

Indians had been using this gesture for literally decades. This move was used to signify something very old and very much of this precious earth. Big Red again adjusted his chin-strapped headdress.

"Then Rascal all yours," Big Red proclaimed, "and Rascal then find lover."

Stinker looked back over to Bongo, who only sneered.

Wow. That is one mean ol' rattlesnake . . .

There wasn't much to do.

Except to say no to Big Red and for all of them to be on their way. Rascal would have to find help somewhere else.

Hey, he did what he could. Right?

But that was too easy . . .

"You're on," said Stinker.

Big Red gasped.

Stinker slipped on his pair of special monogrammed slot-machine gloves that he used whenever racing or making outdoorsy love. No one knew why. Regardless, they were magnificent, what with their anti-slip, pimpled-rubber grip.

"Let's race!"

Jumbo cheered and made homoerotic motions to Bongo, who looked confused.

Boner now launched into his hilarious sports announcer's voice: "What we have here, ladies and gentlemen, is only the finest match-up in the history of car racin'! Oh, I *do* say this is going to be a classic!"

Then Boner, knowing full well he was earning laughs, slipped seamlessly into his Howard Co-Smell imitation:

"What an *invigorating, revitalizing* situation," said Boner. He sounded Semitic, with all of the mysterious and dark forces that came associated with that tribe.

"This situation is *impressive*! This situation is *staggering*—"

Boner stopped. Those were the only long words he knew.

Maybe later.

Buck, who was sitting on the ground banging sticks, exclaimed, "Piss!"

Even the Indian had to laugh at this one. "Piss," this ancient warrior mumbled, breaking into a wide grin, chopping in a downward motion toward his groin with his plastic 'hawk.

"Piss!"

The race was on!

Chapter 27

DOUBLIN' DOWN!

"Affirmative," said Orville, hanging up the public payphone.

$75,000.

Incredible!

That's what the old man's halfwit secretary had said.

Orville had never touched so much money at once.

Had never even *heard* about so much money at once.

Time to double down.

Orville Max III hadn't given up. He wasn't the type of bunglenut to suffer from a nasty case of "defeatism."

Far from it.

If anything, this straight-laced former military man who still believed in the goodness that a barely democratic government could potentially bring to the world's yellow people had only increased the intensity of his mission.

Kicked it into a new, ferocious gear.

Semper Gumby. Always flexible.

Orville jumped into his Cadillac and turned the volume up. A fat broad was singing in a European language about the thin and weak. He loved it.

Before long, Orville was cruising at top speed down the back roads of this magnificent nation, avoiding any and all major thoroughfares.

According to the radio, the main roads were all clogged with Stinker's fans. Orville didn't own or use a CB. That was for the lower-class. Morons. Stupids. Fools. Academics who created their own sand art. Lesbians in pant cuffs who believed in the power of toe socks and Indiana yoga. A vanful of "unsuals." Civvy fartlickers who owned creek rocks as household pets.

Three more hours to Washington. Orville wondered if his former home had changed in the years since he had been helicoptered out at the last minute with the great one before the angry mobs had charged.

Orville was about to enter his old city and wait. And *then* pounce on Stinker.

Orville leaned back, driving with one hand, and thought about intergalactic medical experiments.

Chapter 28

TOIL AND TROUBLE!

The race was over.
Or almost.
Stinker had it locked.
Or nearly.
The stadium was filled with hundreds of thousands

of onlookers, all cheering wildly for their dirt-covered red-necked rapscallion, Stinker. There were a few fans rooting for Bongo. Maybe ten thousand. But not as enthusiastically.

Buck was by Stinker's side. He was wearing his old-fashioned motoring goggles and a funny safety helmet over his coonskin cap but no seatbelt. Stinker liked to call the helmet a "brain bucket," but with the way he drove, the kid didn't *need* no seatbelt.

One hundred and ninety-eight laps, with only two to go.

What a race!

Stinker couldn't wait to hand over to Rascal a ripe chimp of the male variety. Maybe that would finally soothe the ol' girl's savage Amazonial needs. She was too hungry. Too *thirsty*. The primal force of Rascal's lust annoyed Stinker. Just gotta stick that burning spear into a bucket of cooling water. Watch it sizzle. Maybe even take some Polaroids. Later use the photos as "sheet music" for his "skin flute." He'd see.

Stinker was now driving with his knees, touching up his hair in the rear-view.

The car was as close to driverless as an automobile would ever get.

Stinker took the final turn on 198, grooming his eyebrows. He wanted to look exceptional when he stood on that trophy stand, accepting the fancy plaque that would read "#1 AMERICAN WINNER!"

Stinker's trailer was already packed with trophies and plaques and even a few stolen, deflated Mylar balloons reading "FELIZ QUINCEANERA!"

Also, a framed $100 check for having won the 1971 National Strutting Championship.

Quite a few pickled genitals, too. And rare glossy professional stripper photos—framed!

Oh no! BUBBLES!!!!!!

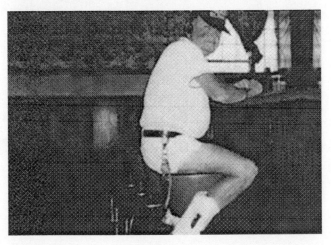

'Twas Nasty Sam!

Rascal ain't so tough around kids!

The black in the crowd!

Stinker's truck-drivin' momma . . . the Million Miler, Charlene!

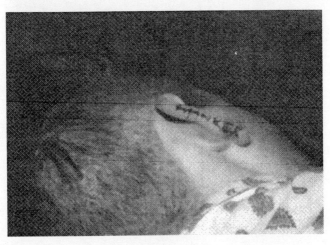

Young fan with a Stinker ear tattoo!

Waiting impatiently for the incredible once-in-a-lifetime race!

Bert and Jilly, the Terrible Truckhouse Twins!

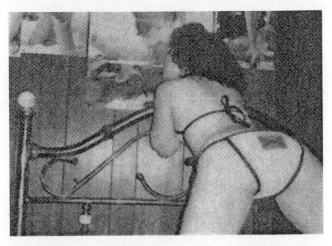

Stinker's spicy lil' firecracker of a special friend, Lizz!

Girls can ALSO drive trucks!

Semi-retarded mountain boy Buck!

"To hell with the typical, boring suburban life! Ride on this stink!"

Some of the orphans!

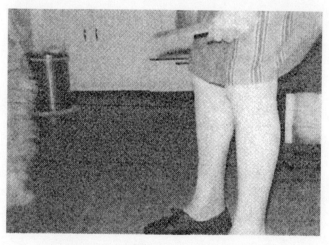

Jeremiah Moses King in drag at the orphanage!

The gyrocopter!

"The Hunk"

Down with "cagers"!

Mary the Canary with her canary, Marie!

The watermelon truck!

"Hey, Ma! It's *this* big!"

Silverweed in a "mood"!

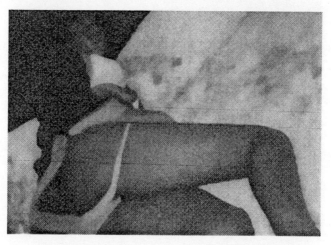

On the road, *anything* is possible!

The gorgeous Dallas Cowboy cheerleaders!

Stinker's second and fourth wife, Maybelline!

But there was *always* room for one more award. His Mema had once told him this just before she fell dead of a heart attack while taking a breathalyzer test in the seashell parking lot of a Lexington, Kentucky Sizzler.

Bongo was way back at lap 196.

This race, as the experts might have said, was in "the wrinkled bag."

"How you going to celebrate?" asked Stinker to Buck, who looked as if he was already celebrating with a bottle of fancy Champagne.

The kid was smacked.

Stinker opened his window and floored the accelerator.

The noise and smells of the spectators entered the car. Stinker stuck his gorgeous nose up as far as it would go in order to take it all in. He could live of off these fumes, morning, day and night—

Stinker screamed.

And then screamed again, a loud, hollow sound devoid entirely of life.

There was only one thing on this here ol' earth Stinker was afraid of . . . and that was . . . believe it or not . . .

. . . *BUBBLES* . . .

And Stinker was *deathly* afraid of them!

To the point where he would cry if he ever saw a bubble. Stinker never cried. Except for that one time when his childhood dog was run over and killed by a car driven by an underage driver.

The driver was Stinker. His middle-aged teacher lover was in the back, nude, clutching her bloody forehead.

It was definitely a *story*.

But here was just one lonely bubble somehow finding its way into the car, floating in from the outside, no doubt from a child's toy or from the *Playboy* bunny photo shoot taking place within the track's midway.

The *Playboy* theme was "Ring Them Southern Belles."

One white playmate was bending over a plantation-era whipping post pretending to be "lessoned."

It was adorable.

"Why of all things a *bubble*?!" Stinker yelled, near tears, and Buck—now awake—could only laugh.

The bubble was glistening with many colors, just like a rainbow. As innocent and harmless as you please! Even a child wouldn't have been scared of it!

Not Stinker, though.

A few years back, when Stinker was a younger man, one of his numerous roadside lovers had asked him about his fear of bubbles. Stinker hadn't answered. He was too ashamed. But the reason was simple. When Stinker was a baby his momma had fallen into a vat of bubbles and nearly drowned. She was a long-haul trucker, having traveled more than one million miles in just one year, back in '56. The first woman to have ever done so.

But she was careless and liked her silly sauce too much. She found herself one long evening in a revolting juke joint on the far reaches of Jackson, Mississippi. A man named Lemonaid had given her a bottle of his own homebrewed honky hooch. It was way too powerful—almost *magical*.

Wandering through the power lines behind the bar, Stinker's mother fell into a cesspool. An albino hermit by the name of Easy Squeazy found her and saved her life by reaching over with his prosthetic leg and pulling her out. On the prosthetic leg was a tattoo of a lucky shamrock. Squeazy was not quite right in the head and had strange sexual thoughts about women and vats full of bubbles.

It was a bad way to go. Mom's ashes now sat in a bedazzled cremation urn inside Stinker's trailer. The urn was an emptied Sanka can.

Stinker shuddered just thinking about it. It was a common story but it upset him just the same. And his father? Found dead after that clothing-optional prison root canal.

Stinker blew at the bubble, which floated ever so delicately over to Buck's side.

Now it was Buck's turn to blow the bubble, this time back over to Stinker. Buck found all this hysterical.

"*Fuck* bubble! *Suck* bubble!" the boy cried out in an idiotic, sing-song voice. "*Cock* bubble! *Cunt* bubble!"

Oh, ain't you havin' fun, thought Stinker, taking his eyes off the road, if only for a brief second.

But it was too late.

Stinker grabbed onto the wheel with both hands and yet he was already in a spin, fish-tailing back and forth on the dirt racetrack. Smoke was billowing from out of the motor.

Something was clearly wrong.

From over his left, Stinker could see Bongo pass.

Bongo was now only *one* lap behind.

Miss Becky came to a hard stop by the side of the track, facing backwards.

The bubble rested ever so gracefully on the bristles of Stinker's mustache. And then it popped.

"Goddamn bubbles!" screamed Stinker. "I *hate* bubbles!"

Stinker put the hammer down by stepping real firm on Miss Becky's accelerator.

Just like she *liked* it.

Nothing.

Stinker must have exploded a rod in the engine during that last nasty spin. He could fix it real fast if only he had the chance . . . but not now.

Stinker slapped the stick into Reverse and then back into Drive, and then slammed down the accelerator.

Nothing.

Reverse and back into Drive. *Accelerator.*

Again nothing.

There's only one thing to do, thought Stinker. *But . . . Stinker don't reverse.*

Stinker never reverses, thought Stinker. *Stinker never has . . . and never will.*

Ever!

Stinker looked straight ahead. Bongo was approaching quickly in his magged-up, superchromed, duel piped, four on the floor 1971 Dodge Charger. One more lap and he'd be the winner.

Unacceptable.

What should Stinker do?

"Stinker DON'T reverse. Ever!" he yelled, almost as if trying to convince himself with the volume of his own beautiful, haunting words.

But then came a slow-motion image of Rascal running through a junkyard, hand in hand with her new chimp lover. Each was holding a rubber enema bulb in the shape of a heart. It was adorable. Strange. But adorable.

That was all it took.

Stinker waited for Bongo to get closer.

Their eyes locked.

Stinker noticed that there was a look of fear in Bongo's huge, moony peepers.

Stinker goosed Miss Becky's hammer, still in Reverse. Accelerator to the floor. She bucked backwards and stopped. Girl wasn't in a mood to groove.

There was only one thing to do: Stinker stuck two fingers in his mouth and let out a whistle. Through the crowd Rascal came galloping. She did not look happy.

Within moments, Rascal caught up to Bongo's speeding auto and hopped easily through the driver's side window. What went on inside, no human should ever see, Stinker included. So he averted his eyes.

Buck, meanwhile, saw blood and flesh and perhaps an elbow. He smiled. It was funny.

Bongo slowed to a quick stop well before the finish line. Stinker let out another short whistle and a tow-truck arrived, hooked itself up to the front of Miss Becky (Miss Becky's front was a *fine* one) and towed it across the line.

The spectators had never seen anything like this. Was such a thing even possible? Less than ten years back, man had first landed on the moon. Seemed impossible then. But compared with this, the moon landing was no more impressive than an early-morning powdered breast milk run to Cleveland.

Stinker flashed the victory sign. The crowd went beserk.

A *Playboy* bunny waved and flashed her luscious porn fritters.

Stinker glanced over to Buck who had already finished the victory Champagne.

Little fucker always was a hog, thought Stinker and laughed.

Buck vomited.

Stinker would get some bubbly later.

All in a day's work.

Chapter 29

HANDING OUT GIGGLES!

The gang stood around Boner's truck and watched the entire rig violently shake. Whatever was going on inside was loud and boisterous. Angry. Messy. Against nature.

Big Red the Indian had been true to his word, unlike most Indians. He had graciously presented Stinker with a trophy for his remarkable win and then with a 23-year-old male chimp named Ole Joe.

This was very old for a chimp.

Rascal's yellow eyes had flared when she first caught sight of Ole Joe. Her privates grew red and inflamed and then began to emit a musky odor that reminded Boner of a supper of red hots roasted with wire hangers over an indoor fire. To Jumbo, the odor was reminiscent of that fetid "secret fold" he had never told anyone about, stinkin' like a week-old slice of tater-tot casserole.

The new primate couple had retreated—more like *exploded*—into the back of the truck to begin their most primal dance. The truck's shimmying started slowly but quickly grew faster and faster until Stinker feared that the entire damn thing would tip over.

And wouldn't that have been a shifty kick in the ol' leather shorts?

The gang waited patiently for the monkey rutting to finish. Boner was afraid that Ole Joe—no spring chicken—wouldn't survive the encounter. Boner had noticed quite a lot of gray speckled around Old Joe's mouth. *Hang in there, ya old Romeo,* thought Boner. *Don't go down for the count!*

After one last grand shake, the truck came to a sudden lurch . . . and then all was silent and still.

"Time to *go*," announced Boner, wasting no time.

"Agreed, *kimosabe*," replied Stinker, using his one Japanese phrase. He jumped into Miss Becky without opening the door. He had already fixed the broken rod. Actually, he had paid a Spanish to do it for him. Truth be told, he wasn't the "best" around engines.

Stinker gave Big Red a fake tomahawk chop.

Red grinned.

This savage was *unusually* easy to please . . .

Stinker looked over to Bongo, who grimaced . . . but then smiled , even though he was horribly disfigured and missing an elbow. Even this large galumph was taken with Stinker's natural charm and charisma. Or perhaps Bongo still suffered from that brain injury he experienced as a toddler at the hands of his seven-year-old aunt, Mindy.

Stinker pulled out of the circus entrance and then onto the road leading north.

"Breaker, breaker," Stinker heard from his CB transmitter. It was Boner. Even though they had just spoken seconds before, it was vital to constantly communicate via the ol' citizens band.

"This here be the Stinker," said Stinker. "Go on!"

"Son, it looks like you got yourself some fans," said Boner. "This highway is lined sweaty ass deep, boy!"

It was true—and then some. Seemingly millions of men, women and children lined the two-lane highway. This was no surprise.

For it was now clear that it was Stinker that this country so desperately needed in these fantastically difficult times.

In the past decade, the economy had become unglued. There had been wars. Corruption. Macramé. A granny-glasses-wearing freak with a figure-skating haircut who sang about "mountain mommas."

Chaos.

Madness.

But then here arrived this everyday, mildly out-of-shape hero named Stinker who, without complaint, attempted to deliver urine-colored, convenience-store, American-produced garbage beer to the President of the United States.

In his previous evening's broadcast, Walter Cronkite had even used the term "far out."

That was a first.

Far out, indeed.

By the side of the road, good old American commerce was being taken to the extreme: Stinker T-shirts, Stinker buttons, Stinker CB mic grips, Stinker-shaped sex toys. Stinker wondered if he'd ever see a dime from these earnings. Probably not. But this new-found fame could only help when it came to funding future amazing adventures.

Anything could happen now.

Soon enough, Stinker saw the inevitable: a male streaker with an exceedingly hairy pubic region running through the crowd, the 13 colony American flag draped over his narrow, furry shoulders.

This was American patriotism at its best.

A few miles away, Stinker saw a rock and roll band

called The Shag Reflex. By the sounds of it, they weren't singing about Stinker at all, which was disappointing. From what Stinker could make out, the band was warbling about marijuana, which was all well and good, but Stinker still preferred alcohol and red pills brewed up by the good ol' Doc.

Pure. Not god-awful, hippy garbage grown in a back field manured to the moon by slippy dippy stink. Why fly to heaven if you could "hop" there?

At another point, just South of Leesburg, Virginia, Morganna the Kissing Bandit had jiggled her way from out of the crowd and directly over to Miss Becky, where she leaned in and kissed Stinker smack dab on his sumptuous lips, which caused Gwyneth to become at first jealous but then a little sad when she realized that kissing was Morganna's entire life.

Was this any way to live?

Stinker had one arm around Gwyneth's seat, enjoying the ride. Buck was busy in the back seat making spastic motions with his hands and filthy feet.

War-Shington existed just before them.

Nothing else stood in the way.

To his left, Stinker saw a miserable man in a station wagon filled with a wife and three kids.

To his right, Stinker saw a half-dead gentleman in a business suit who looked to be on his way to work.

Suckers. Nothing but straight-laced, caged suckers!

Stinker was in heaven, practically home free.

Or . . . almost . . .

"Wondering if we have time for a quick detour?" Boner asked suddenly over the CB.

Gwyneth looked to Stinker.

No way, her expression seemed to say. *Let us just get to Washington already and deliver this darn beer to the President! No more adventures for this fancy girl!*

"What you got in mind, ol' boy?" asked Stinker, ignoring Gwyneth's look.

"A quick visit to the orphanage," said Boner. "We drop off and bolt."

"I like that," said Stinker, grinning. "We hand out the giggle items at cry land for the short short and then smack on down the road. Come back, come back!"

"See you there, good buddy," said Boner. "Ten in the wind. Brevity breaky-break on the six nine!"

He cut off.

"Are we headed to an *orphanage*?" asked Gwyneth, who wasn't quite fluent in the language of high-end CB communication.

"Always try to," said Stinker, as if it was no big deal. As if every heroic warrior on I-95 took time out of haulin' beer to provide very cheap toys to sad, forgotten orphaned children for very small tax write-offs.

Gwyneth began to cry. She had never met anyone quite like this mysterious Southern beast. Raw but tender. Ignorant in world matters and yet brilliant when it came to useless CB lingo. Hairy without officially needing medical intervention. Possibly deranged in a very masculine, 1970s way. Arrested frequently but never officially convicted with a felony.

"I do think I love you," said Gwyneth, tenderly touching the back of Stinker's head.

"Ha ha!" laughed Stinker. His laugh was very distinctive. It would have sounded strange coming from just about anyone else but a man who owned a camouflaged carpal-tunnel splint.

"You really think you can tame this wild coon?" asked Stinker. He was talking about himself.

"Never fell in love with a *raccoon* before," said Gwyneth, impishly. Her eyes twinkled. She was now double parked in his erogenous zone. "Let alone a *wild* one."

Stinker pulled over to the side of the road.

He had urgent business to handle in the woods.

And it involved Gwyneth.

He grabbed his slot-machine gloves.

Gwyneth followed.

It was impossible not to.

Chapter 30

KISS OFF!

The little man and his sheriff daddy were still awkwardly propped by the side of a South Carolina road.

It didn't take long for a brave trucker to arrive to douse them both with glue.

A few minutes later, another brave trucker arrived to tar and feather them.

The two flatfoots became an emblem for all the hatred the great working white men in this wondrous country had been experiencing over the past decade.

The little man spat out a feather and said, "*Harrumphaadsta.*"

The big sheriff daddy spat out an even bigger feather and responded with the equally nonsensical, "*Sssssssuppparuuuuuf.*"

Within the next few hours, plenty of other truckers and looky-loos arrived.

By that evening, both the sheriff and the little man

were made to resemble two members of a popular rock and roll group far more famous for their makeup and tongue size than for their awful, screechy music.

Tourists took photos. Children threw trash. A stew bum named Tic Tac urinated against a fence post and passed out.

A toothy Japanese television crew arrived and began to nod and giggle and cover their mouths whenever they found anything amusing, which was predictably often.

It was all very funny.

The Americans on one side, doing their north American thing.

The nips on the other, catching it all on film, raffling rike clazy . . .

Charlie off the wall, ding dong!

Chapter 31

WHERE ARE THEY?

All of the Christmas toys and boxes had been wrapped. There were seemingly hundreds of gifts, all stacked neatly to form a giant pyramid in the orphanage's grand foyer.

There was just one problem.

There were no *orphans*.

"What gives?" sputtered Jumbo, upset.

The fat man loved his kids and, for the most part, they loved him back.

Except for that one child, the one he never talked about. That kid in Indiana, a state he was no longer allowed to travel through. Or even fly over.

"Don't know," replied Stinker. "Usually the obnoxious whelps wait for Boner and I. And then Mr. Walsh, the owner of this orphanage, he's usually right here. This don't smell right."

It really didn't. And this time, you couldn't blame the odor on Jumbo. Or his "secret fold" that now stunk like raccoon gravy that had roped in the heat.

Just then, from out of one of the grand entrances, walked a man Stinker didn't recognize.

"Hello," said the man.

Instantly, Stinker didn't trust him immediately.

"Hello," repeated the man, smoking a long cigar. "My name is Jeremiah Moses King and I am the new owner of this here beautiful orphanage."

"What happened to Mr. Walsh?" asked Boner.

"And the kids?" added Jumbo, concerned.

"They'll be looked after just fine," said the man, not concerned, puffing away.

Cuban, thought Stinker. *Just has to be a Cuban . . .*

Gwyneth stepped forward. "Sir, I am a mathematician—"

The man looked at her as if to imply, *Yeah. Right.*

" . . . and what you are now telling me," Gwyneth continued, "does not really . . . *compute.*"

Stinker smiled.

This dewy-eyed doe was going to long outlast this year's beaver hunting season.

No need to throw her back into Poon Pond.

She was a keeper.

"And why is that, little lady?" asked the man with the long cigar.

"I will tell you why," exclaimed Gwyneth, with great confidence. "Because if the kids are truly okay, then why are all of their little shoes still here?"

She pointed to the corner.

Sure enough, there, in the corner of the orphanage's grand foyer, was a pile of children's shoes. There had to be well over two hundred.

Stinker felt a cold electric current course down his macho spine. *Gwyneth was right. Something was truly off.* And it wasn't just that he still didn't understand what Gwyneth had said earlier about computing.

Jeremiah King's smile faded. "Because . . ."

He paused.

"Trying to think of a fib?" ejaculated Boner.

The smile returned. "Because . . . because I bought all of these fancy shoes just after the kids left."

Boner looked over to Stinker.

The man was obviously lying. But how to prove it?

"Have to hit the head," announced Boner suddenly. He was using a military term for *bathroom*. Boner had never been in the military, but he found it cool to pretend otherwise.

"What are the coordinates?" asked Boner, all military like. He also had never been in the military but loved stories about POWs stuck for years and years inside bamboo cages.

"Down the hall to the left," said Jeremiah.

"Want to join me?" asked Boner to Stinker.

"You two *funny*?" asked Jeremiah.

"About as funny as Big Foot in a leisure suit," replied Stinker, grinning.

Jeremiah didn't laugh. His "Big Foot IQ" was in the low range.

Jeremiah turned around and then got down on one knee. He leaned toward Buck, eye to eye. "Hey there, kiddo! How are you?"

Buck hissed.

Stinker had never before seen this type of reaction from the kid. A lot of other crazy reactions, especially around bath time, but nothing like this.

Jeremiah stood back up. You could tell he wasn't so great with children by the way he almost burned out Buck's eyeballs with his lit cigar.

"Anyway," Jeremiah continued, "the kids are all fine and I thank you for stopping by with their Christmas presents. They will be enjoyed very much!"

Stinker wasn't buying it. It was garbage. Stinker *never* purchased garbage. Except once. But in his defense, he had been plenty wiffy off indoor paint fumes.

"Where are they?"

"Who?"

This man was *not* good at playing dumb.

"The kids, goddamnit!" yelled Stinker, who rarely yelled, especially within an orphanage. "Where are the orphans I come to see every year for a tax write-off?"

As Jeremiah was about to answer, he was cut short by Boner calling from the other room.

"Think I found 'em!" Boner called. "Get in here, quick!"

Stinker and Gwyneth went running. What they saw next stunned them. *Stunned them beyond belief.*

All of the orphans were crammed shoeless into a small room, blinking back against the bright light now pouring in thanks to Boner having opened the door. With his arms around to protect them, Mr. Walsh also squinted back with fear.

"Oh, *thank god*," said Mr. Walsh. "*Boner and Stinker!* If it wasn't for you, I think we'd all be *dead!*"

Boner nodded.

The guy had a point.

"*Got* him!" yelled Jumbo from the foyer.

Stinker and Boner and Gwyneth ran back into the foyer and found Jumbo sitting on Jeremiah King.

The cigar smoking man wasn't going *anywhere*.

"Get off me, ya big lard!" screamed the man.

"Get me some rope, Stink!" declared Jumbo.

Although not great at taking orders from those who were fatter, Stinker did as he was told.

The man with the cigar was soon tied tighter than a rodeo clown just out on parole.

"You're a hero, Jumbo!" yelled Stinker. "You're a damned fool and you're way too fat . . . but you're a *hero*!"

Jumbo blushed. It was all true.

"Finally earned your keep, big boy," said Boner, slapping Jumbo on his ample, fleshy back. "I apologize for ever thinking what I thought about you earlier."

"What did you think earlier?" asked Jumbo.

"Oh . . . you know . . . nothin' . . . that was . . . *too* bad," Boner replied and everyone laughed.

While they were laughing, Jumbo looked sad, but brightened quickly when a just-freed orphan approached clutching a large candy cane.

Jumbo and the child went off to the corner to mingle. The rest of the pink-cheeked orphans surrounded Stinker and Boner and Gwyneth, and began their story.

The story they told was absolutely *incredible*.

Chapter 32

DID I JUST HEAR RIGHT?!

The story was over.

It had to do with Jeremiah wanting to tear the orphanage down in order to build a huge roller-skating rink.

"A roller-skating rink?" Jumbo had asked. The thought of Jumbo on roller skates was both adorable and a bit horrifying.

"A roller-skating rink," confirmed Mr. Walsh. "Can you believe that? With *disco* music."

"Incredible!" farnicated Boner, who hated disco music more than just about anything, including homosexual urbanites who danced to that type of slinky, frictionless music that lasted way beyond necessary.

"But we're not out of the woods just yet," said Mr. Walsh, watching Jeremiah being led away by the police.

"If we don't come up with $25,000 by Christmas," continued Mr. Walsh, "we will surely be shut down for good."

"$25,000," burbled Jumbo. "That's . . . that's a lot!"

"It is," said Mr. Walsh, solemnly. "We tried earning it ourselves but it was impossible. We tried *everything*. Bake sales. Car washes. . . ." Mr. Walsh trailed off. He seemed tired. "We even contemplated having the children earn extra cash by doing some cleaning over at the Mulligan Street halfway house but . . ." He didn't finish. It wasn't necessary. Just the thought of his orphans being forced to clean an above-ground plastic hot tub filled with sex infections made everyone a bit sick.

Boner and Stinker looked at each other. There was an unspoken communication between these two. They were like two wild dingoes noticing each other on the Austrian Outback from a great distance who knew instantly—without any doubt—that they both very much wanted to smell each other's undercarriages.

There was only one thing to do.

Stinker spoke first. "Mr. Walsh. I've been coming here for many years now. I first met the orphans when they were children. Most are now grown. Hell, I probably even unknowingly slept with a few." He stopped for the laugh. When none came, he continued:

"But," he continued, "there are probably many thousands out there now, lining the roads, streaking nude while wearing a red, white and blue Uncle Sam top hat. I see the goodness you've done. And because of that, I feel that I have no choice . . . "

He's not, thought Jumbo. *No way in the world! The man is cheaper than a rabbi on vacation!*

" . . . but to give $2,000 to your orphanage. That'll at least get you started."

"What?" said Mr. Walsh, not quite believing it. "Did I . . . did I just . . . did I just . . ."

Get on with it already, thought Stinker.

"Hear right?" Mr. Walsh finished at last.

"Not now," Stinker explained. "I can't afford it now. When I return from Washington after having completed my mission. You can have it *then*. *If* I complete my mission. And *if* I return from Washington. And *if* I'm paid in cash. Or paid *at all*. Then."

The tears flowed freely down Mr. Walsh's cheeks. He, like everyone else in the country—no, the *universe*—had been religiously watching the news each and every night. That a man this brave and cheap could offer such a ridiculously generous offer—even if it was a worthless IOU, not close to anything that would truly help—was beyond the realm of anything that Mr. Walsh had ever heard or witnessed, including his own very recent kidnapping.

"I . . . I don't know what to say," spurted Mr. Walsh.

In the corner, Buck—softly at first, and then more loudly—began to chant.

"What's he saying?" asked Jumbo, turning away from his new orphan friend and still eagerly sucking on his candy cane, now down to just a nub. "Don't know if I've heard this one before."

It took everyone a few listens but it soon became apparent.

"Can't be!" said Boner. "Just can't!"

"I think it *is*," said Gwyneth. "I think this is *really* happening!"

Stinker listened even more closely. There was no doubt. *Could there be any doubt at all?*

No. The kid was actually saying it!

And what Buck was saying, was the following:

"Love."

And then again "love!"

And then one more time, even louder . . . crystal clear: "Love!"

Gwyneth was beside herself with joy: "He's not cursing anymore! Buck is talking only about *love*!"

"Well, I'll be damned," said Boner, taking off his

cowboy hat and slapping it against his thigh. He did this whenever excited or arrested.

"Stinker, you *broke* him," said Jumbo. "You broke that lame feral creature but *good*!"

Stinker was a bit more circumsized than his friends. "I reckon I din' do nothin but teach him about the *real* world. A world where there are no Jews or Negroes or Italians or Octoroons or honkies or half-breeds or Injuns. There are only people—people just like you and I—who want to do good and ride the straight and arrow. As opposed to those who are bad, who tussle in the mud that's filled with the toxic hate that's still crawlin' within 'em. That's all. That's all I reckon I done."

Stinker had impressed himself with the depth of his own speech, even though he himself had tuned out midway through.

"It really is about *love*," said Boner, spreading his arms out wide. "I heard all about love from the original trucker in that good ol' book of his. Hell, if that Big Dog himself had a CB radio, he'd *still* be talking about it!"

"Jesus?" asked Gwyneth.

"No," said Boner. "He was good. But I'm talkin' about the guy who wrote *The Complete CB Handbook*."

Boner grinned playfully.

Mr. Walsh stepped forward and whispered something in Stinker's ear.

Stinker nodded sadly.

After a pause to collect himself, Stinker announced: "Mr. Walsh thinks it might be best to leave Buck here. With kids his *own* age."

Stinker was doing his very utmost to try to keep it together but it wasn't easy.

"Hey, kid!" Stinker said. "You okay with that?"

Buck finally looked up.

"*Love.*"

"That settles it," said Stinker. "You ain't going no-where. You stayin' right here. I brought you out of the mountains to break you. My job is now done. But, boy, you better not go drinking up all the Champagne! Leave a little for your ol' man!"

Buck smiled. He would never forget what Stinker had done for him—namely getting him hooked on booze at a very young age.

"*Love,*" the kid said again.

Stinker rolled his eyes. He was growing a wee bit tired of the word "love." *How many goddamn times could he hear it already?*

It really was time to leave this shithole and bring this amazing adventure to a colossal close. Time to magic.

Chapter 33

THE D OF C SLOG!

Founded sometime in the 1800s, Washington D.C. was—and still *is*—a swamp.

Everyone knows it, even those who choose to live in it.

President John Kennedy once said something fun-ny about the city being more northern than Southern and more Southern than northern but—as was often the case with Kennedy—the quote was never written down, so no one knows exactly what was said.

Regardless, Washington is a city filled with mean men who don't look like our boy Stinker. That is, hard-working, blue-collars who can easily accomplish manly acts of heroism with their own callused hands.

Those who might not know the best word to use before a Supreme Court bailiff but who are extremely adept at changing the oil in their three-wheeled golf carts with balloon tires, or who are more than capable of hanging a hilarious "NO DUMPING" sign above the toilet, or who can easily steal a chimpanzee from a circus and get away with it—at least for a few months.

Washington is a city that does not exactly welcome men like Stinker with open arms and fancy placemats. Or Jumbos. Or Rascals.

And, yes, even Boners.

But Stinker didn't play that game. He played by his *own* rules . . . rules that were now going to allow him to take this half-northern, half-Southern city by storm.

To take control.

To make it his *own*.

With all this in mind, Stinker and Boner were parked just outside the White House gates, engines revving.

Stinker walked over to a pay phone. Slipping twenty cents into the slot—two nickels and a dime—Stinker waited for the operator to pick up.

One eventually did: "Washington D.C. May I help you?"

In his best Southern "no-way-in-the-hell-will-she-ever-be-able-resist-this-adorable-cottoned-honeyed" voice, Stinker soothed: "Hello, little lady. This here be the Stinker. I'm thinkin' right now that there might just be a lightning-bug flash in Dixie you've heard of me and my exploits?"

The operator—no stranger to dealing with the world famous—responded with, "Maybe."

Stinker liked a challenge.

"I think you're playing coy."

"Maybe I am then."

"I think you know who I want to talk with."

"Whom," said the operator.

"The President," said Stinker, growing impatient.

"And you want me to patch you straight through?" asked the operator, just as impatient.

"I do, indeed," said Stinker, stroking his 'stache, literally dripping in this horrifying summer humidity.

This was hell itself. And Georgia summers were supposed to be the worst . . .

"And what makes you think that I patch through every yokel who wants to speak with the President?"

Stinker was growing frustrated. He liked this operator's spunk but not her intelligence. He hadn't envisioned it ending like this.

"I don't think you understand," said Stinker, trying to be patient. "I am on a mission to deliver to the President a six-pack of Schlitz. And I have to do so before tonight."

"That so?" the operator asked.

"That so," answered Stinker, at last fed up.

"That so," the operator replied, and hung up.

Must be a lesbian, thought Stinker.

He made his way back over to Miss Becky.

Gwyneth was growing impatient. "Are we going to meet the President or *what*?"

What lip! Women and their nerve storms! Maybe this relationship wasn't going to work out after all . . .

"I said I would and we will," pronounced Stinker.

Could he get a goddamn break here or what?

He grabbed the CB mic and keyed it three times, the signal for Boner, only a few yards away, back in his truck, to pick up, which he did.

"Got no other choice here, Bones," said Stinker. "Let's break down them thar gates."

"Not enough backup," said Boner. "Just I and you, brother. We'd need a *lot* more than that."

Stinker thought about arguing but then looked at the guards manning the gates.

They did *not* look like they were fooling around.

In fact, they looked as if they just might be crazy enough to shoot innocent, hardworking, white, *real* Americans.

"I'm at a loss here—" started Stinker but then stopped.

Was he hallucinating?

"Am I hallucinating?" asked Stinker into the mic.

"No, sir, you ain't hallucinating," replied Boner. "You most definitely ain't hallucinatin'."

It was incredible.

In the distance, from just over the marbled horizon, a fleet of semi–trailer trucks was rumbling their bad-ass way straight to the White House.

It was a blue-collar workingman army, ten thousand strong.

Or *twenty* thousand!

It was denim revolution time.

And it was glorious!

Chapter 34

DOWN IT COMES!

The wrought-iron gates came down quickly.

It was virtually impossible to stop a semi from ever doing what it *wanted* to do.

No. What it *needed* to do.

The White House soldiers—who had never seen *real* action—fired their guns uselessly in the air as a sort of warning, but then quickly fled.

They were little match for this band of Southern road-bandits and they knew it. Scampering off into the night, they would end up out of work but at least they were alive.

Lucky.

Jumbo screamed with delight. He was on the White House grounds! He wondered if the place had a good cafeteria with plentiful hot-chocolate enemas.

Boner pulled the cord for his truck's horn. He launched into yet another character, one he was particularly infamous for among his friends and probation officers: the crazed weatherman. "I think the forecast calls for violence!" he announced in his best jarring northeastern accent. "And I do believe it's going to be stormin' up some serious Boner and Stinker!"

Jumbo pumped his chubby fists. He still felt good about pulling his excess weight back at the orphanage.

Maybe he wasn't a fat, worthless toad after all?

Boner's truck came to a hard stop in front of the main door to the White House, where so many of the world's important leaders had grandly entered over the years.

Now here came perhaps the *finest* leader of them all: Stinker . . . along with his frayed crew of rag-tag Southern dingleberries.

Boner exited the truck and joined Stinker and Gwyneth in front of Miss Becky.

All three confidently walked directly into the White House as if they owned the place.

In a way, they already did.

Chapter 35

GOVERNMENT WEEKNESS!

"May I be of any help?" asked an officious-looking man in a foreign suit with thin and effeminate lapels.

Boner had seen this type before. And knew how to deal with it.

"Affirmatory," Boner replied, confidently. "We are here to see the President of the United States. We are here to hand over to the President . . . *Schlitz*."

Stinker held up the six-pack of Schlitz still bundled

in its fancy gift wrap but now out of its cardboard diaper box.

"I'm impressed, really I am!" announced the government official. "This is a *beautiful* six-pack. And Schlitz, my absolutely favorite!"

Stinker seriously doubted this guy ever drank beer, let alone Schlitz. Looked more like a wine guy . . . a wine *spritzer* guy.

"But I'm afraid," the man continued, "that the President isn't here. So I will have to accept this most gracious gift on his behalf."

"Where is he?" asked Stinker, patience running thin.

No way in hell was he just handing over this precious cargo to a worthless paper-shufflin' jack-off-demic . . .

"At the ballpark," the toadie announced. "About to throw out the first pitch at the annual All-Star game."

Jumbo went into a full wind up and pretended to throw a fastball. He practically fell on his chubby face.

It was funny.

The worthless bureaucrat continued: "If you'll allow me, I can certainly take charge of this here ol' six-pack and make sure that the President most definitely do receive it."

The man was trying without much success to speak Southern.

In D.C., you were either wonky or honky.

It was clear on which side of the chicken fence this idiot fell.

"Not happening," said Stinker, making the motion for his minions to do an about-face and drive on back through the White House's entrance. "Ain't buying into any of your Buddha jujitsu bullshit."

"Are you sure?" asked the white-collared man. "You could just simply hand it over."

"And no one would ever see it again," said Stinker.

He hopped into Miss Becky.

"I may be a backwoods Billy Bobble Dobble but I ain't stupid," Stinker declared as he revved the Trans's engine and squealed her around the White House's circular driveway, leaving tracks.

Had that ever been done before?

(Stinker Jr. would one day read about it.

And be incredibly impressed.

That is if there *was* a Stinker Jr.

And if the kid dug history and could read.)

Stinker noticed in his rear-view that the President's pathetic assistant was shaking his tiny fists in impotent frustration. It'd be a long day in hell before anyone could pull one over on the Stinker.

Those fragile fists never saw a tough job in their lives.

Stinker got back on the mic. "My fellow truckers," he said. "Until I return, I need me some brave apaches to guard the big house. Come back, come back. Who's got the jewels colossal enough?"

"You got yourself a hero," said a voice over the CB's speaker.

"And who might that be?" asked Stinker.

"This here Nasty Sam," said the voice. "And for the Stinker, *anything*."

"As would I," announced another voice over the CB's speaker.

"As would I, too," announced yet another voice.

The voices were now coming in fast and furious.

"As *would* I."

"As would *I*."

"*As* would I."

Thousands strong, each enunciating a different word, but essentially saying the same thing: that the revolution could not be stopped.

Would *not* be stopped!

Especially by a college-educated, European-dressed, government-sponsored ninny who drank woman wine and who shook feeble fists at an unmovable blue-collar force.

"Ten-ten, till we do it again," announced Stinker. "We're down and gone. So long, comrades!"

Stinker was talking to his army:

Pooty Stank.

Mello-Hello.

Big Grab.

Catnip.

Shaitan.

Master Bang Bang.

Doctor Twitch.

Shazam.

And, yes . . . even a lone female:

Miss Sprinkles, Dyke Dynamo X-Treme.

Unmovable. Strong. Unified.

It was *magnificent*!

Chapter 36

STRAIGHT SHOT!

Stinker had a straight run to the stadium. His fellow truckers made sure of that. It was like a private road that only Stinker could use, buttressed on either side by thousands of trucks blocking the way. Stinker felt as if he was finally in paradise.

If this ain't heaven, please don't show me hell, he thought. He giggled in that strange way of his. He couldn't help it. He was irresistible, especially to himself. He gave himself a mental handshake. The grip was strong.

Without traffic, the ride took no more than thirty minutes. As Stinker passed each truck, a horn would sound, a continuous, victorious bleating that lifted Stinker's spirits as he made his way toward what he could only assume would be the toughest part of the entire mission.

Was the President going to be cool? Or a shithead? A stand-up regular guy? Or a Gucci-wearing ass who only ate French onion soup? With crewtons?

Stinker had a pretty good idea that this was far from a sure thing. But he also knew that in many ways he'd been preparing for this particular challenge his entire damn life.

All of those illegal beer runs across state borders. All of those seemingly impossible missions for the Big Man, like that time delivering Pop Rocks to legless Vietnam Vets for Christmas.

Unfortunately, the vets also tended to be toothless.

All those endless nights spent dreaming of one day delivering metallic-tasting, sub-par yeast water to world leaders for seemingly and apparently no good reason—but it didn't matter.

It was finally *happening*.

Pinch me, thought Stinker.

"Look!" shouted Gwyneth, pointing to the sky. "A man in a *hang glider*!"

Stinker looked skyward. Sure enough, floating above them all was a bearded man without a shirt and wearing very loose cotton track shorts. He was giving Stinker the thumb's up. Stinker shot one back.

"Wait. That's not a thumb's up," said Stinker.

Gwyneth blushed. *That was most definitely not a thumb's up. Just a very loose pair of shorts . . .*

Stinker pulled up to the entrance of the ballpark and hopped out. Gwyneth followed, throwing Stinker a nasty look for not opening her door. Stinker caught the look and wasn't happy.

This really might not work out after all, thought Stinker. *What a pain in the goddamn ass . . . plus, she's really starting to show all of her thirty years . . . ridden hard and put away wet . . .*

A security guard was waiting for them.

"Ain't gonna happen," the guard said, before they even approached.

"Oh, you gotta be kidding me," replied Stinker, exhausted from all of the "nos" and none of the "Yes, Stinker, *follow* me!"s.

"Just ain't gonna happen," repeated the guard.

"Not through *this* entrance. Or *any* entrance," he added. "You will not *walk* into this stadium to meet the President."

Stinker pulled back his fist as if to punch this loser but was stopped at the last second by Gwyneth. She made a motion with her head. *Follow me.*

You sure you know what you're doing?, Stinker motioned back.

Just follow me, she motioned.

Woman, are you sure?, Stinker motioned in return.

As sure as I'll ever be, Gwyneth motioned in response.

But are you sure? motioned Stinker.

I'm tired of motioning, Gwyneth motioned. *Can we stop this?*

Stinker motioned: *Yeah.*

Away from the guard, Stinker asked: "What gives?"

"He just told us that we can't walk into this stadium," said Gwyneth. "Isn't that right?"

"So?" said Stinker, not following.

"So there's another way," she replied.

Gwyneth looked up.

Stinker followed her gaze.

And there *was.*

Chapter 37

AND AWAY WE GO ...

Rascal was calm.

Oh, was she calm.

Stinker had never seen the ol' girl so calm.

If chimps smoked—if chimps were like 12-year-old mountain boys—she'd be sucking back on a Pall Mall right about now. The look in her eyes was complacent.

Not a care in the world.

Bring it *on.*

That is until the hang-gliding helmet was forced onto her head and she was strapped into the flying contraption fashioned from out of laminated fabric and flimsy stainless steel.

"Now, everything is gonna be alright, girl," said Stinker, trying his best to project calm. "Just fly on down from the top of this here stadium and hand the President this six-pack. Okay? And then run off. *Real fast like.* I'll be waiting for ya up here!"

Rascal looked sadly at Stinker.

"And then you can see your pal Ole Joe! That's what you want, *right?*" said Stinker.

Rascal didn't say a word but she did allow for a big, sloppy hug from Jumbo.

The gang was standing on the roof of the baseball stadium. They had climbed up with the help of a hidden, unused fire-escape Gwyneth had located by paying $10 to a middle-aged usher named Benny. To Gwyneth, Benny had looked "a couple bubbles off plumb."

"Rascal," said Gwyneth, soothingly. "I promise that when all this is over, I will make you whatever dessert you want! Coconut cream pie? Banana cream pie?"

Rascal said nothing, but she didn't argue. Banana cream did sound mighty good, even if she wasn't so hot on digesting lactose. Gave Rascal the "staggers."

Before she knew it, Rascal was already strapped into the hang glider. The bearded man who owned the contraption stood just off to the side, counting the cash Boner had paid him: $15 in singles. His shorts were still very loose but he was no longer flashing a "thumb's up," which Gwyneth was grateful for.

It now looked more like the "curse finger."

"Anything I should tell her?" asked Boner to the man. "Any advice?"

"Just don't die," said the man. "Really, the fall ain't too bad. Till you hit the ground."

"A comedian," mumbled Stinker. "Everyone's a comedian."

And then with more pep in his voice, Stinker said, "Okay, Rascal. We all set now?"

Rascal's helmet was all askew. She looked silly.

Stinker handed the girl the Schlitz.

Rascal grabbed at it absent-mindedly.

Boner thought: *If this jungle wench had any gee-damn idea of how much this six-pack of Schlitz is worth . . .*

"Listen," said Stinker, placing a red jacket vest on Rascal. "Take this if it'll make ya feel better. You can wear it! It's my good luck puffer vest!"

Stinker zipped it up, and then patted the chimp's strong back for good measure. "Will keep you warm during the fall."

With that, Stinker gently pushed Rascal off the roof—Rascal whimpered and let out a horrified cry.

Stinker looked down to see whatever fate might befall this chimp, this troubled creature he loved more than practically any other female primate in the world.

He put her chances at half and half.

Not bad.

Chapter 38

FIRST PITCH!

"Ladies and gentlemen, would y'all please rise and welcome to the field, the President of the United States! Mr. President will be throwing out the ceremonial first pitch!"

To Stinker and the rest of the gang, this announcement sounded no better than a series of echoes. But Stinker got the idea. He could see—*barely*—the President striding confidently to the pitching mound and, with his fancy dress shoes, digging into the dirt like a real baseball player. He started his exaggerated windup and went to release the ball . . .

But there was an audible gasp from the crowd, and thousands of fingers were quickly pointing skyward . . .

The President finished his windup and hurled the ball towards the plate. It did not make it, bouncing well before the catcher, who was also looking skyward. The catcher scooped up the ball and ran back to the President.

The President was only now noticing a screaming and blaring chimp strapped into a hang glider, wearing a dented and used helmet, flying directly at him with great speed. To the President's expert eyes, it did not appear as if the animal knew how to control a hang-glider.

Somewhere between Georgia and Washington D.C, Clarence MacLeod sat alone on his leather throne, on the top floor of the tallest building South of the Mason Dixon, observing all of this—*live*, for crying out loud!—on his brand-new 85-inch, black and white deep-set television.

Was that a goddamn monkey flying a hang-glider? Where in the hell is Orville? Please, dear Lord, I'm not a begging man, but I am begging with you today: I beseech you to never allow that six-pack of Schlitz to reach the hands of the President of the United States!

Clarence then leaned forward. Did he just use the word "beseech" correctly?

Meanwhile, back on the baseball diamond, the President stared slack-jawed at what he saw approaching rapidly from above.

The man had seen a lot in his fifty-odd years.

Things on a Navy battleship—typically in the boiler room—that they never talked about in recruitment pitches.

Blights that decimated millions of dollars worth of runner peanuts and other priceless legumes.

An alcoholic brother with a penchant for stripping

nude and using a neighbor's trampline without permission.

But *this*?

No, he had *never* seen anything quite like *this*.

What goes on inside the mind of a President of the United States?

No one knows—not even the Presidential experts.

Maybe not even the Presidents themselves.

But perhaps it goes something like this:

President going to die!

President killed by chimp strapped into hang-glider!

Chimp holding six-pack of beer?

Why?

From way up above, looking down, Stinker could see that the chimp was directly on course, heading straight for the President, but way, *way* too quickly. Perhaps he shouldn't have pushed that damn hang-glider off the stadium roof with such force.

Or at all.

Jumbo, Boner and Gwyneth were leaning over the edge of the stadium, watching intently. Jumbo was rocking nervously. Boner was praying. Gwyneth, of course, was crying. So much hinged on what happened next.

And what happened next, no one could have ever predicted.

Not even one of those mythical one-eyed gypsies with an uncanny "second" eye.

Chapter 39

SECOND THOUGHTS!

The first to react on the field was not the President of the United States but rather the secret service men who had been trained for just such a circumstance.

The men burst forth with machine guns, all aimed at Rascal.

"Do not fire!" screamed the toothy President. "It's a chimp! And it's holding a six-pack of beer!"

The lead secret service agent put up his hands. "Halt!" he screamed to the rest. They did as they were told. That was their job. Unlike back-road warriors, these soldiers were *very* adept at taking direct orders.

The crowd cheered. They could now see for themselves that this wasn't a Russian assassin.

It was nothing more than a chimp in a hang-glider, clutching a six-pack of beer.

And, most amazing of all, the chimp actually seemed to be leveling its hang-gliding craft and slowing it down. Whether it was due to Rascal's spastic arm and leg movements or just out of sheer luck couldn't be determined.

Rather, it was a very funny sight.

The crowd began to laugh.

The secret service agents soon joined them.

And within no time, the president was also laughing.

His laugh was annoying, grating and liberal.

Rascal was now coming down for a soft landing, just yards from the mound. A professional hang-gliding instructor who was human and male could not have achieved what Rascal was achieving. Smooth. Controlled. Level.

Sublime.

The crowd began to applaud.

But a shot rang out!

The secret service agents—no longer laughing—suddenly leaped toward the President, shielding the leader of the free world with their bodies, leading him briskly off the field. He appeared stunned. *Did this ever happen to Lincoln?*

The baseball players who had all been so eager to bound on to the field now retreated back into their dugouts. They weren't so *heroic* now . . .

The crowd's attention turned to the chimp who had just fallen with a great thud onto the field.

"It's been shot!" someone screamed.

"It's dead!" yelled another.

A security guard ran towards the great beast. "I see a bullet hole!" he yelled, making a desperate motion for the paramedics to move faster.

The crowd gasped.

"What are they saying?" asked Stinker, from above.

"Not so sure, good buddy," replied Boner. "But it don't look good. No good at all!"

Down on the field, the security guard ran a finger across his throat to signify *This chimp is dead.*

The crowd roared its collective disapproval.

The secret service agents would have joined them, but they were gone. So was the President.

All was quiet. And this is when Orville Max III chose to leap on to the field, as if from out of a slit trench, clutching his M-16 rifle.

Orville wasn't wearing a shirt.

His face was painted green and white.

He was wearing a gook headband.

He was busting it tiger style.

Bookoo bad.

Chapter 40

A SCREAM …

"Orville," Stinker muttered from his perch high up above. "Orville Max! I haven't seen this tightly-strung deviant since '73. We were racing to deliver tainted lunch meat to the same Georgia elementary school in broken refrigerated trucks!"

Stinker smiled at the pleasant memory. [See *Stinker Cannonballs Into the Ass-End of Insanity,* 1973]

"That bastard killed our Rascal," said Boner. "And now I'm gonna kill him, too. But not just yet."

"Well, what are we going to do?" asked Gwyneth with a girlish tremble in her voice.

"We just wait," said Stinker. "Sometimes you just gotta wait."

"How can you possibly be so cool?" asked Gwyneth.

Stinker didn't even need to answer. He was *that* cool.

Down below, there was no movement from Rascal.

Things weren't looking good.

Orville sprinted full-speed at the chimp, grabbed the six-pack without checking to see if the animal was even okay, and then ran back toward the dugout—

—which was now being blocked by the baseball players with their bats. Orville tried the other dugout, which was also blocked.

He wasn't going *anywhere*.

Maybe these baseball players were braver than they at first appeared? Not as brave as football players, but certainly a lot braver than soccer players, a game Orville never understood or liked. Why so popular in Europe?

Gay.

Orville preferred *classic* sports, such as nude olive-oil wrestling with army buddies . . .

Orville was in a panic. Holding his rifle in his left hand and the six-pack curled beneath his right, he attempted to burst over the small wall that divided the field and the crowd.

The crowd stood cross-armed.

"You lily-livered, leftist ninnies!" screamed Orville. He aimed his M-16 straight at a blonde-haired young girl no older than eight. "Let me in! Or I'll shoot her! *And I'll do it, too!*"

There was a scream. And then thousands of heads turning to look to the mound.

Rascal was slowly lifting herself off the ground.

She was alive!

"But how—" started Orville, also turning.

Up above, Stinker smiled.

It was that red down-vest he had given the ol' girl.

Bullet-proofed for maximum enjoyment.

It had done the trick. Just like Stinker knew it would.

As Walter Cronkite might have said just the other day: "Far out!"

On the field, Orville cocked his rifle and re-aimed at the young child. "Let me outta here," he practically spit. "Or I'm gonna shoot this kid! *I mean it!*"

He smiled and it was chilling.

"I've killed children before. Over *there*," he made a motion with his head to the east.

The *far* east.

The crowd parted. Orville leaped into the aisle and disappeared without hesitation into the thrumming throng of thousands of tenacious baseball enthusiasts and their tittering tots.

And, just like *that*, this immaculately-dressed man with the black carnation was gone. A white apparition in a dense human jungle.

Chapter 41

UP, UP AND …

The President had been brusquely ushered out of the stadium and into his limo.

Stinker had failed.

There wouldn't be $10,000 to pay for a new trailer toilet.

There'd be no $2,000 to have to give to the orphanage. Which was good. But that $10,000 . . .

Stinker had failed.

Stinker.

Had.

Failed.

Stinker sounded that sentence out in his brain.

Failed.

Stinker.

Had.

It sounded like another language. Impossible to understand. Stinker had never heard those particular words strung in that order before. Or in any order. He didn't like the sound of it.

But it wasn't all bad, right?

On the upside, he was an international star, famous throughout the country and the entire world for his heroics and bravery and numerous inappropriate knick-knacks lodged in his copious lady tickler.

On the downside, he'd still have to urinate out of his kitchen window whenever he was too drunk or jammed-up off the reds to leave his trailer.

Stinker was kneeling on the field now, holding Rascal ever so gently. The chimp had opened her eyes and had smiled when she first saw Stinker. Her breath was horrific but Stinker was okay with that.

He always was.

"C'mon, girl," he said sadly. "Let's get you back in your circus chains in that shit-smelling truck and haul your fat ass home to that trailer you hate so much."

It was touching.

Stinker and Rascal stood and the crowd roared its approval. With great difficulty, the chimp put her injured right arm around Stinker's shoulder and was led to the dugout. The players formed a line on either side and placed their caps over their hearts.

It was a sign of great respect.

The crowd was on its feet, showing Stinker and Rascal just how much they appreciated their great effort—even if they *had* failed.

Sometimes just trying was enough.

It was the American way.

And at least the beast was alive—if horribly maimed. This was no act. This chimp would never again perform somersaults at a circus for the honor of not being whipped by a one-legged trainer with "anger issues."

Gwyneth stood to the side weeping, of course. There was even a tear or two in the eyes of Boner. As for Jumbo, he was eating a frozen Swanson turkey dinner with all the sad trimmings. Typical fatty behavior.

It's a shame this didn't work out, thought Stinker. *Could have made for a hell of an ending.*

A great noise could suddenly be heard.

At first Stinker thought it had to be coming from Jumbo, perhaps suffering from yet another heart attack. Or stroke. He was up to three this week.

But the noise was coming from above.

From a hot-air balloon!

"What *the*—" began Stinker.

But Rascal already knew.

It was the same hot-air balloon that she had ridden earlier!

The pilot must have seen her on television and flown straight to her rescue!

The balloon landed behind second base with a soft sigh.

Rascal cast her yellowed eyes on the pilot, who reached out to once again haul her on board.

And then along came Stinker, Gwyneth, Jumbo and Boner.

"Are you sure we'll be safe?" asked Gwyneth, from inside the basket.

"We really have no choice," replied Stinker, a bit perturbed. "Just deal with it."

She really is a lippy broad.

"But . . . I *afwaid*, so very *afwaid!*" Jumbo said and everyone laughed.

"No, I'm *really* afraid," he continued, this time without the fake childish speech impediment.

They still laughed.

Boner was more confident. It was a confidence emanating straight from Stinker, as well as the two beers he had consumed since hitting the field.

"I know what I'm doing," replied Stinker.

Then, to the pilot, Stinker gave the thumb's up.

The real one. Not the one in his extra-tight jeans.

And up they went.

Chapter 42

"WHY, HELLO DERE! MIND IF I DROP IN?"

Orville sped along the Beltway that encircled the city of Washington. Seated next to him, in the Cadillac's passenger seat, was the prized six-pack of Schlitz.

Orville imagined himself walking straight into Clarence MacLeod's office and plunking this treasure onto the old man's fancy veneer work desk like you would the head of a dead enemy solider.

Long ago, Orville had actually done this. Didn't work out like he had hoped. Then again, this was at IRS headquarters. And the head belonged to a neighbor.

As far as this fantasy . . . Orville would pop open a can of fresh brew right in front of Clarence and have himself a relaxing drink. Might even sleep with that big-breasted blondie right there on Clarence's desk with Clarence watching and Wagner playing with himself. Or the blondie watching and Wagner playing with Orville.

Nonetheless, it would be lovely.

"Lovely" wasn't a word Orville used often. Except once at a Bangkok back-alley cock-fighting parlor named The Horny Moon, and even then under extreme duress: gun to his pink, knife to his stink.

Suddenly, there was a huge bang . . .

At first Orville thought the car's rear windshield had been blown out. He then realized that the noise was coming not from behind . . . but from *above*. Steering with one hand, he leaned his head out the driver's-side window and looked up.

It was a hot-air balloon.

Resting on his car.

Could this be happening?

It all felt so surreal. He had been so goddamned close to escaping the heavy gravitational pull of his former city . . .

Stinker was standing on top of Orville's car that was moving at 75 mph.

It was a miracle for the ages. Big Red would one day be telling his little red grandpups all about it, complete with fancy Injun gestures and elaborate smoke rings.

Then, with one seamless move, Stinker was securely inside Orville's car, sitting in the passenger seat, all cool-hand juke.

"Give me that six-pack, Orville. And nothing happens."

The six-pack was now sitting on Orville's lap.

"And if I don't?"

"And if you don't . . . " Stinker paused. "Then we *all* pay the consequences."

"Who's we?" asked Orville.

"This entire country," said Stinker.

"Meaning?" asked Orville.

"Meaning we come from two sides of the same coin," said Stinker. "How much is your boss paying you?"

"*My* business," replied Orville. "That'd be entirely my own damn business."

"*Our* business," said Stinker. "Let's say we pool our money and then split in half? Then we're *both* happy."

Orville thought about this. "I don't do business with enemies."

"And what enemy might that be?" responded Stinker. "A salt of the earther scraping together a living on cracked pavement rather than expensive leather?"

"What's the matter with leather?" Orville asked.

"Makes my ass sweaty," replied Stinker, grinning. And then, growing more serious: "We've had our differences, right?"

"Right," agreed Orville.

Well at least Stinker was getting *somewhere*.

"Like that time you tried to stop me from carrying crates of donated kidneys out of Six Flags."

Orville giggled. "*Ooooooh boy.* Turns out they *weren't* donated . . ."

"Or kidneys," Stinker finished. Now it was *his* turn to giggle.

Stinker was on a roll: "Orville, you and me, we each love this country. We love women."

Orville kind of shrugged.

"And . . . men," said Stinker, a bit reluctantly.

Orville brightened.

Stinker got himself a good third wind:

"We hate smokeys. And we hate . . . what else? Oatmeal? You prefer grits, right?"

Orville was perplexed but had to admit he did.

"Just think how powerful we could be if we ever decide to join forces. *Think about it.* In the meantime, hand over that there six-pack."

Orville clutched the six-pack even more tightly to his groin.

"Orville," Stinker said patiently. "Hand it over. *Please.*"

Orville sighed . . . but did as he was told. When

Stinker asked nicely, no human on earth could resist, even a Vietnam vet with the post-war "scrambles."

"Anywow," said Stinker all cool, climbing back through the passenger-side window and out onto the roof, "it has been *fun*, as always."

Stinker grabbed the dangling rope attached to the hot-air balloon with the hand not clutching the Schlitz.

And Stinker flew onward toward his destiny.

Chapter 43

NEXT TIME!

Little Man and his sheriff daddy were still propped up by the side of the road and probably would be forever.

Tourists stood around, thousands of them, gawking, each signing their names onto the plaster casts, taking photos, laughing, pointing.

Mocking.

Little Man just rolled his tiny eyes.

Next time.

He'd get Stinker next time.

He spat out a feather. And looked directly at the camera and then at you, the reader. He shrugged.

It was really funny.

Chapter 44

HANDOFF!

What goes on inside the mind of a President?

No one knows.

And yet Stinker was about to find out.

The President's limo was driving through the White House gates and around the circular driveway. It came to a hard stop in front of the main entrance. Stinker could see all of this from high up above. He made a flamboyant motion to the pilot to land the balloon on the White House's East Lawn. The pilot did so without question and everyone was soon on the ground.

The reception was not exactly a *welcome* one.

"Hands in the air!" screamed a secret serviceman. "*Now!*"

Jumbo put his hands high into the air and urinated his large pants.

The secret serviceman couldn't help but snicker.

Who was this fat man? He was amusing.

"Now let's just all calm down," said a voice from the limo. Stinker couldn't see the face behind the voice but he could tell by the distinctive Plains twang that it was none other than the most powerful man in the world —not including Stinker himself.

"Approach," said the voice. "But *only* Stinker."

He knows my name, thought Stinker. *The President of the United States knows my name!*

The hairs on Stinker's hirsute forearms sprung forth erect. So did the hairs in his nostrils. He had the chills.

"This way," said the voice. "Just follow my voice. Don't be afraid."

Stinker walked alone over to the limo, past all of the armed secret servicemen. One winked. *Must be one of the few good ones . . .*

"Stay right there," commanded the voice coming from the limo.

Stinker stopped a few feet away. He still couldn't see the President's face.

"I've heard that you would like to hand me a six-pack of Schlitz," declared the liberal-inflected voice.

"That would be true," said Stinker. "And I have it right here for you."

"Is it cold?" asked the voice.

"*Cold*?" asked Stinker. "Cold *enough*, I guess."

"That wasn't my question," said the voice. "I asked if it was *cold*."

Do you know what I've been through to get you this six-pack? Stinker wanted to say. Instead he asked, "Do you know what I have been through to bring you this six-pack?"

"I don't," said the President. "But then again, that's not my problem."

"So what you're saying," said Stinker, "is that I can't hand over this here six pack? The one I practically dragged up straight from hell?"

"Not unless it's *cold*," replied the President.

Stinker thought, *Guy's not nearly as straight-laced as we thought.*

Stinker felt the sides of the cans. They were lukewarm. Definitely guzzable. But if the leader of the free world wanted them super cold, then it looked as if Stinker had himself a *problemo*.

Out of the corner of his masculine eye, Stinker saw TV trucks and newspaper reporters pulling up. He could also see that they had begun shooting with their fancy Oriental cameras:

Crick! Crick! Crick!

And he had been so damn *close* to finishing the mission. Couldn't he just sprint over to the limo, throw the stupid six-pack at the President, and then make a run for it?

True, he was out of shape and his elbow was still horribly "off" from a tractor accident inside the locker room at an all-girls Catholic school [see *Stinker Loses a Pinkie*, 1971] but maybe? . . .

Or maybe not.

Stinker wasn't sure.

Stop asking so many goddamn questions!

Stinker shrugged and began walking over to the hot-air balloon.

Maybe the colorful aircraft will fly me all the way back to Georgia. I won't have to pay off the Trans Am's lease. I won't have to worry about fixin' that damn blown-out front windshield. Just claim an owl did it or something. Would have to remove those illegal STNKR69 vanity plates, of course, but that shouldn't be too difficult. Wouldn't have to pay the idiot orphanage a penny.

It's not all bad . . .

All of a sudden there was a very loud *bang*!

A car came crashing through the wrought-iron fence surrounding the White House. It was an explosion so loud that Gwyneth let out a scream, which wasn't surprising.

Stinker also let out a scream, which *was* surprising. He never screamed.

"*What the?*" Stinker exclaimed. He turned.

It was a Cadillac. The very one driven by Orville.

Stinker grinned. And he'd swear on the holy *CB Bible* until the day he died—most likely tooling down the highway, one eye on the road, the other on a *Richie Rich* comic—that he saw Orville grin, too.

Chapter 45

COLD BEER HERE!

The Cadillac screeched to a jarring halt just behind the President's limo. Orville popped out.

He was holding a fresh six-pack of Schlitz.

"Heard you needed a few *cold* ones," said Orville, all cool. He winked.

Stinker winked back. *This guy wasn't so bad after all. They'd make a good team. More alike than they'd ever care to admit. Except for the homo thing.*

"*All* boats rising," said Stinker. "Together we can take over the world!"

They shook hands. Their grips were powerful.

"The pleasure is all *yours*, my friend," said Stinker, motioning to the limo. "Finish it, Orville."

Orville nodded. It was nice of Stinker to allow him to do this. He wouldn't soon forget it.

Orville gingerly approached the President's limo. He wasn't used to seeing Democrats up close. Usually it was through the sites of a rifle. Or begging for their lives in a prison shower.

"Mr. President," Orville began, most humbly, "it is my duty—no, it is my *pleasure*—to hand over to you a most delicious and *cold* six-pack of Schlitz."

Flashbulbs popped and video cameras whirled.

"*Finally*. A gift I can accept," said the President, staying in his limo.

You still couldn't see his face but the simple joy in the President's voice was unmistakable.

His job done, Orville sidled back over to Stinker. They shook again. The grips were just as strong.

Everyone on the East Lawn applauded. Except for the thin-lapelled wonk with the honky pretensions.

Fuck off, Little Lord Fart-Leroy! thought Stinker. *You're playing with the big boys now!*

Stinker laughed. He couldn't help himself.

Somewhere between Georgia and Washington D.C, Clarence MacLeod sat alone on his leather throne, within his office, on the top floor of the tallest building South of the "Masey Dixie," watching the latest satellite news coverage from Washington on his brand-new 85-inch, black and white deep-set television.

He didn't like what he was seeing. Not at all. Then again, he couldn't say he was overly surprised. The whole idea had been a little cockeyed from the get go. He'd find a way to deliver to the President a six-pack of Revive soon enough.

But he'd save that for another day.

Clarence switched over to a rerun of *Green Acres*. It was the episode in which Arnold joined the Hare Krishnas but insisted on eating meat.

Back on the White House Lawn, more and more cars and trucks were arriving through the gates.

"The orphans!" cried Gwyneth, letting out a girlish scream. "They've come to congratulate us!"

It was true.

Mr. Walsh, the orphanage's director, ran towards Stinker.

"How about that $2,000?" he asked jovially.

"What?" Stinker responded, annoyed.

"The $2,000 for the orphanage," Mr. Walsh said.

"Don't know what you're talking about," said Stinker, cheeks growing warm with displeasure.

"We need $2,000," responded Mr. Walsh patiently but looking less jovial, "for the orphanage. Not sure if you remember, Stinker, but you did tell me and the rest of the orphans—"

"SHUT!" interjected Stinker, who very rarely screamed. "FUCK!"

Mr. Walsh sighed and walked pathetically away. He was definitely no backroad warrior.

"And Doc!" yelled Boner. "He come, too!"

It was true. He come, too.

"And Ma, with a heaping slice of her famous apple pie!" sang Jumbo.

That wasn't true. But Stinker was okay with that. Ma was hideous.

"Fuck," said Buck, running up to Stinker for a hug. "Fuck, fuck, *fuck*!"

"Love," corrected Stinker. "It's all about *love*, Buck. Remember that!"

"Shit," said Buck. "Piss, fuck, shit, cock, *pussy*!"

The President let out a laugh. This mountain child was funny. Reminded him a bit of his idiot brother— the type to smoke a cigarette on the groaner while pinching out a live one.

Stinker sighed. The damn kid would never learn, but the important thing here was that the kid was violent when it was needed most . . . and he would be needed most soon enough. No more orphanage shit.

Rascal leaped from out of the balloon's basket and hurried over to Stinker.

The world watched, including the Big Man, who nodded as if he knew the entire time it would end like this. Maybe he did. That's why they called him "The Big Man." And because he was exceedingly large.

Rascal hugged Stinker around the waist. And then, reaching up, she began to lovingly pick out the remaining food items that the wind hadn't carried off.

Within no time, the 'stache was empty.

It was like something from a classic award-winning film. Or a movie playing at a few Southern drive-ins for a couple of weeks in the deepest and saddest part of the summer. Either way, Stinker was a *winner*.

Gwyneth began to weep. It was all too perfect. She thought back on her promise to bake Rascal a banana cream pie and prayed the animal wouldn't remember.

Stinker glanced over to Gwyneth. Maybe he wouldn't throw her back into Cooch Canal after all. Still, it wouldn't be too long until her hair was dyed, fried and laid to the side. Until there was a general sag to her body that would make Stinker wince. Maybe he would *then* throw her back. Either way, he'd wait until the next rest stop to decide.

Rascal galloped back to the hot-air balloon and began to attack the pilot, chasing him around the basket.

It was a gas. The chimp didn't seem to notice that Ole Joe had passed away moments earlier, 'neath the presidential limo, from dissipation.

Don't you get caught, thought Stinker. *Mr. Pilot, don't you dare get caught!*

Stinker and Boner made eye contact. Stink winked. Boner was in no rush to head back to his wife and thirteen children. And Stinker was in no rush to head back to "Harry Pussè." Pet iguanas could live forever. There was just too much fun to be had out on the road. Boner winked back.

Best pals *forever*.

The sun was beginning to set. It was nearly dusk on a Wednesday evening in the middle of July in the year of the Christian Lord 1977.

Here in the D of C, the gang had accomplished what they had set out to accomplish. They had all learned a great lesson these past few days, although they couldn't for the life of them figure out what it might be. Regardless, there would be many additional adventures, sooner rather than later.

Great things were about to happen to America. There was little doubt about that.

But for now, it was time to party. A song could be heard warbling from the President's limo:

That man, he like to ride,
Stinker let's loose!
Stinker let's loose!
That man, he do like his beer,
That Stinker, he don't never hide!
Stinker let loose, Stinker let loose!
Virile, regal, heroic, hairy,
This Stinker, he don't ever find nothin scary . . .

Stinker gave a thumb's up.
. . . except for bubbles!
Stinker made a funny face. And then shrugged.
'Twas the least the great man could do.